THOMAS
JEFFERSON'S
CRÈME
BRÛLÉE

Thomas Jefferson's Crème Brûlée

HOW A FOUNDING FATHER

AND HIS SLAVE

JAMES HEMINGS

INTRODUCED FRENCH

CUISINE TO AMERICA

BY THOMAS J. CRAUGHWELL

QUIRK BOOKS
PHILADELPHIA

TO MY FRIENDS AND
FELLOW FOOD
HOUNDS, TERESA
AND BILL GIBBONS

The publisher wishes to express thanks to Bonnie Coles and the staff of
Duplications Services at the Library of Congress, Leah Stearns at Monti-
cello, and the Digital Curation Services department at the University of
Virginia Library for their help with images for this book.

Library of Congress Cataloging in Publication Number: 2011946051
ISBN: 978-1-59474-578-2
Printed in the United States of America
Typeset in Bembo and Old Claude

Designed by Doogie Horner
Cover illustration by Dan Craig
Editorial assistance and photo acquisition by Jane Morley
Production management by John J. McGurk

10 9 8 7 6 5 4 3 2 1
Quirk Books
215 Church Street
Philadelphia, PA 19106
quirkbooks.com

CONTENTS

Prologue: The Man Who Abjured
    His Native Victuals   1

Chapter 1: Americans in Paris   17

Chapter 2: A Free City   37

Chapter 3: A Feast for the Palate   59

Chapter 4: The Wine Collector and the
    Rice Smuggler   77

Chapter 5: Brother and Sister, Reunited   99

Chapter 6: Boiling Point   119

Chapter 7: The Art of the Meal   139

Epilogue   161

Appendix

    The Wine Connoisseur   169

    Vegetables: Thomas Jefferson's "Principal Diet"   177

    African Meals on Monticello's Table   185

    A Selection of James Hemings's and Thomas
    Jefferson's Recipes   191

Chronology   200

Notes   205

Select Bibliography   222

Index   230

Prologue

THE MAN WHO
ABJURED HIS
NATIVE VICTUALS

About five in the afternoon of May 7, 1784, not long after dinner had been served at Monticello, Thomas Jefferson sat down to write a brief note to his friend and protégé William Short. "Congress have to day," he wrote, "added me to the commission for negotiating treaties of commerce with the European powers."

News had just arrived from Paris that one of the commissioners, John Jay, was sailing back to America, leaving the team one member short. Jefferson would fill the void. He had not yet booked passage or begun to pack, but already Jefferson's ever-busy mind had an inspiration about what he might accomplish in Paris, and he was not thinking about commerce commissions. "I propose for a particular purpose to carry my servant

Jame with me," he informed Short. "Jame" was nineteen-year-old James Hemings, one of Jefferson's slaves. And the "particular purpose" was to apprentice James to some of the finest chefs in France. Thus began the most interesting and influential culinary partnership in American history.

We know Thomas Jefferson as a political philosopher, an amateur naturalist, an ardent gardener, a zealous bibliophile, and an inveterate tinkerer. But he was also a serious gourmand. Researchers studying Jefferson's papers have found notes detailing the salting and curing of pork, the steps necessary to make a great cup of coffee, and the reasons why the basis for all soups should be raw meat and butter. For fifty-eight years Jefferson kept a Garden Book and a Farm Book that recorded myriad details of plantation life, including what was grown at Monticello, how the crops fared, and when the produce was ready for his table. These documents reveal that Jefferson, whom many consider the most cerebral of the founding fathers, was also a man of the senses, one who was governed by his taste buds.

Like all food hounds before and since, Jefferson collected recipes, and more than 150 of these have survived. Many are variations on early American comfort food, like catfish soup, beef stew, and apple dumplings; such dishes were known in Jefferson's day as "plantation fare" and surely formed part of the meals served at Monticello.

His decision to have James trained as a French chef tells us that Jefferson, who was interested in just about everything, was also curious to learn more about the celebrated cuisine of France. Exactly when he became interested in French cooking is a mystery—he had no opportunities to sample refined Continental cooking while in the United States. There were no French chefs in eighteenth-century Virginia; most cooks were enslaved Africans or free blacks, a fact that may account for the African influence in much Southern cuisine and explain the presence of such ingredients as okra and sweet potatoes, which were transported to the New World on slave ships. French colonists were present in America, however—mostly Huguenots (French Protestants) who settled mainly in Massachusetts, New York, Pennsylvania, Virginia, and South Carolina. Like every other immigrant group, they brought their culinary traditions to the New World, but they never introduced their country's *haute cuisine* to the American colonies. In fact, they disdained it, as did their English and Scotch-Irish neighbors, whose opinions resembled those of eighteenth-century cookbook author Hannah Glasse. In her 1784 book *The Art of Cookery Made Plain and Easy*, Glasse dismissed French cuisine as "an odd jumble of trash" and denounced "the blind folly of this age that would rather be imposed on by a French booby, than give encouragement to a good English cook!"

The mainstays of American colonial cooking were primarily meats (boiled, roasted, baked, or stewed), breads, heavily sweetened desserts, and generally overcooked vegetables. An archaeological excavation at the Virginia home of the rabble rouser and rebel Nathaniel Bacon uncovered piles of bones from such diverse animals as chickens, cattle, pigs, sheep, deer, and rabbit as well as duck, geese, quail, and passenger pigeons. Nothing out of the ordinary among those items. But archaeologists also found the skeletons of turtles, catfish, sturgeon, bear, and even a bald eagle. Most surprising were the remains of frogs. Bacon's varied diet was probably representative of what other colonists ate, too.[1]

Like their English counterparts, early Americans preferred their foods seasoned with garden herbs. Clove, nutmeg, allspice, and cinnamon were available, but their high cost made them prohibitive to most cooks and caused spices to be used sparingly in colonial kitchens.

Fresh fish appeared on the table from time to time, but, aside from sturgeon and oysters, seafood dishes were not popular. The earliest settlers in Massachusetts were especially scornful of fish—a fact all the more extraordinary in a place where the nearby ocean teemed with cod, flounder, haddock, and sea bass, and the rivers, lakes, and streams flowed with trout, pike, bass, and catfish. When the Pilgrims gathered fresh, succulent clams and mussels, they invariably fed them to their pigs. The tidal pools near Plymouth were brimming with lobster, but the Pilgrims regarded the flavor of these crustaceans as bland and uninteresting. In his journal for the year 1622, William Bradford, governor of Plymouth Colony, recorded the landing of a ship filled with settlers from England. The arrival was a thrilling event, yet Bradford confessed that he and his fellow residents were humiliated to have nothing better than lobster to offer the newcomers.

The Puritans of Massachusetts were devoted carnivores, and they shared the Native Americans' taste for wild game— the English had enjoyed venison and rabbit in the Old World, and deer and hares were abundant in the New World as well. The local tribes also introduced the English settlers to baked beans. The natives mixed the legumes with maple syrup in an earthenware pot, added a large piece of fatty bear meat, and then set the pot in a pit lined with hot stones to bake for several hours. The colonists adapted the recipe to suit their tastes: they preferred molasses as a sweetener and substituted salt pork for bear meat. The result was a dish that has become a New England classic. Food folklore tells us that throughout the eighteenth and nineteenth centuries, Saturday night in Boston was "baked beans night"; recipes for this hearty dish can be found in the oldest surviving Yankee cookbooks.

The Indians also introduced the European settlers to corn, which immediately became a staple of the colonial pantry. Later in Virginia and other colonies with large enslaved populations, corn took on particular importance. Because the primary cash crop on plantations was tobacco, a labor-intensive plant that required near-constant attention, the enslaved field-workers were forced to toil from dawn until dark six and a half days a week. Consequently, few slaves had time to tend their own gardens or to hunt or fish to feed themselves and their families. It fell to the plantation owners to provide their provisions. And since human labor was a valuable commodity, most masters took care to feed their slaves healthy food. Indian corn became the keystone of the slaves' diet.

Native to America, corn was readily available and easy to grow. Best of all, it was remarkably nutritious. This fact was made clear when some planters began replacing their slaves' rations of corn with wheat. Soon thereafter the slaves were noticeably weakened, their powers of endurance diminished. Planter William Byrd recorded that his slaves "found themselves so weak that they begged to allow them Indian Corn again." When George Washington tried replacing corn with wheat, he found that his slaves, "in order to be fit for the same labor, [were] obliged to have a considerable addition to their allowance of meat."[2]

It was during the American Revolution, when France sided with the colonists against the British, that American officers first encountered France's culinary flair. The cooks in the French army adopted an American classic, roasted turkey, but enhanced it by adding truffles to the stuffing. The French even added corn mush sweetened with molasses to their menu, a staple of the American frontier that they improved by adding a shot of cognac to the recipe and topping the dish with whipped cream. Despite this promising beginning, the French alliance had no lasting impact on colonial cuisine. As late as 1796, when the first American cookbook was published in Hartford, Connecticut, author Amelia Simmons declared, "Garlicks, tho' used by the French, are better adapted to the uses of medicine than cookery."

After the revolution, some American tastemakers promoted plain food as a virtue. Cookbooks emphasized simplicity and frugality, not meals that brought a succession of interesting flavors to the table. French cuisine was openly derided as foppish and fancified—unworthy of honest, down-to-earth, straight-forward, plain-speaking Americans. Patrick Henry, who became one of Jefferson's foremost political antagonists, once publicly denounced the epicure of Monticello as a man who had "abjured his native victuals."

The "native victuals" of Virginia in the late 1700s were undeniably homey, but they were also served in abundance. Breakfast might include freshly baked bread, corn pone, pancakes, cold ham, chicken, and several types of hash, washed down with tea and coffee. Dinner was heavy on meats, especially when guests joined the family for the evening meal: baked ham, roasted turkey, boiled mutton, and roast beef, plus raw oysters, many vegetable dishes, and salad tossed in a vinaigrette dressing, with nuts, puddings, stewed fruit, fresh fruit in season, and perhaps calf's-foot jelly for dessert. On special occasions or holidays such as Christmas, the menu might include roast pig. The idea was to display hospitality by offering guests virtually anything their hearts desired.

Jefferson was as gracious a host as any member of Virginia's plantation aristocracy. In August 1773, his wife, Martha, recorded that in the space of three weeks and two days, the household and their guests had consumed "6 hams, 4 shoulders, 2 middlings [of bacon] . . . 3 loaves of sugar in preserves, one ditto in punch." Clearly, Jefferson did not scrimp when it came to entertaining, but he disliked the wasteful, excessive choices that were the hallmark of traditional plantation fare. He pared down his menus, an economy noticed by at least one of his houseguests. During Jefferson's final years, Margaret Bayard Smith, wife of the editor of the *National Intelligencer*, stayed at Monticello. She could barely conceal her disappointment when all she was offered for breakfast was "tea, coffee, excellent muffins, hot wheat and corn bread, cold ham, and butter."

The lavish "groaning board" Smith missed had become a tradition in English America. What the colonists had in abundance was food, and they loaded their tables with a rich variety of dishes as both a token of hospitality and a sign of their personal pride in the richness of the New World. At another Virginia home, Smith would have found several varieties of meat and fish from which to choose, along with soup—often more than one—fresh vegetables in summer, pickled vegetables at other times of the year, bread, puddings, and fruit preserves. The food historian Katharine E. Harbury points out that although many differences separated the upper and lower classes in colonial Virginia, the menus of both were virtually identical. The same meats and vegetables served at a stately plantation home could also be found in the cabins of a frontier farmer.[3] The only difference was in the preparation: the gentry favored elegant sauces and had house slaves who could make them, whereas a woman on the frontier lacked the time and income for such luxuries.

Virtually all the settlers of colonial Virginia were English born or of English descent, and they possessed an almost overwhelming desire to be as refined and sophisticated as their families and friends back in England. Household inventories show that the plantation aristocracy collected linen tablecloths, fine china, and silverware, including forks, a relatively new implement in seventeenth-century Virginia. Before its invention, diners used spoons, knives, or their fingers to deliver food from their plates to their mouths. The fork had obvious advantages: it was easier to manipulate than a spoon, safer than a knife, and tidier than fingers. Although the Virginia elites adopted the fork, the rest of the colony was slow to bring the innovation to their tables. A study by Lorena Walsh and Carole Stammas reveals that between 1700 and 1709, only between 3 to 8 percent of Virginians owned the tined utensil. By 1778, that number had risen to only 21 percent among the poor and 52 percent among the middle class.[4]

The management of a plantation household fell to the lady of the house. She supervised the cleaning, mending, and laundry. She oversaw the various methods used to preserve food: smoking and salting meat, pickling vegetables, and laying down root vegetables and fruit, as well as beer, wine, and cider, in cool underground cellars. In addition, the mistress planned the meals, ensured the food was prepared properly and served elegantly, welcomed guests and arranged their accommodations, and, of course, saw to the needs of her husband, children, and domestic staff. In common parlance, housekeeping was known as "carrying the keys," a reference to the large ring that held the keys to every room and storage facility on the plantation, which she kept with her at all times. Martha Jefferson would have learned these management skills from her mother, and ideally she would have passed these lessons along to her daughters, Martha and Mary (later known as Maria).[5] But when their mother died in 1782, the girls, called Patsy and Polly in their youth, were only ten and four years old, still too young to have been taught how to supervise all the necessary household-related tasks.

For Jefferson, Monticello was a private mountaintop paradise, and he planned it as such. The house, inside and out, expressed his ideas of beauty, harmony, and perfection. So, too, did the grounds. His gardens were not simply decorative; they produced the fruit, vegetables, and herbs that fed his family. They also served as botany laboratories where he experimented with varieties of fruits and vegetables to discover which ones would thrive in Virginia.

In 1770, Jefferson directed his slaves to cut a large terrace from the side of the mountain behind Monticello and clear the ground for a kitchen garden. In time, this garden would expand to a thousand feet long and eighty feet wide and produce more than three hundred varieties of vegetables. Initially, Jefferson divided the two-acre area into twenty-four square plots and assigned each to grow what he called "fruits," "roots," and "leaves." Tomatoes and beans qualified as fruits, carrots and beets as roots, and lettuce and cabbage as leaves. Along the border of the garden Jefferson planted English peas, his favorite vegetable. Around the entire expanse he had constructed a ten-foot-tall wooden fence to keep out wildlife (especially deer and rabbits) and his livestock. Below the terrace stood Jefferson's orchard of four hundred fruit trees, his vineyard, and his berry garden, in which he grew currants, gooseberries, and raspberries.

Throughout his life Jefferson experimented with different varieties of plants, importing them from Europe and Mexico. "I am curious to select one or two of the best species or variety of every garden vegetable," he wrote, "and to reject all others from the garden to avoid the dangers of mixing or degeneracy." He ordered young fig trees from France, squash and broccoli seeds from Italy, and pepper seeds from Mexico. Meriwether Lewis and William Clark returned from their exploration of the vast Louisiana Territory and beyond with new varieties of beans and salsify—collecting unfamiliar edible plants had been part of the instructions they received from President Jefferson.

Jefferson's orchard—he called it "The Fruitry"—grew primarily apples and peaches, whose bounty delighted him. During one especially plentiful harvest, he wrote to his daughter Martha, "We abound in the luxury of the peach." He also grew other exotic species, including apricot trees imported from France and almond trees from Spain.

It was Jefferson's dream to make fine wine at Monticello, and he ordered cuttings of *Vitis vinifera*, the classic European wine grape, for his two vineyards. Unfortunately, the European vines did not thrive in the local soil. Black rot and infestations of phylloxera, a species of louse that attacks grapevine roots, destroyed the plants. After seven failed attempts to cultivate European vines, Jefferson experimented with hardy American grapevines; these plants were pest resistant, but the wine they produced was unpalatable.

Amid this toil and effort, Jefferson received the invitation to spend several years in France as a commerce commissioner. To a man in love with fresh produce and fine cuisine, the appointment was a godsend, for France in the late 1700s was experiencing a culinary renaissance. The revival had begun the century before, as French chefs moved away from the cookery of the Middle Ages and its reliance on generous dollops of spices and sugar to flavor food. Instead, they turned to stocks and sauces to build layers of flavor, a method that remains the hallmark of classic French cuisine. The new style of cooking skyrocketed to success after being embraced by Louis XIV, the so-called Sun King. Fundamentally, it called for simplicity, but simple dishes could not be served to a monarch. Consequently, meals destined for Louis reflected absurd levels of opulence and abundance. At his palace of Versailles, some 324 servants were devoted solely to preparing the king's meals, which were spectacular even during the penitential season of Lent. In previous reigns all courses had been served at once, crammed on the table or arranged on a massive pyramidal serving structure. Louis introduced the innovation of distinct courses, one following another. Each course left the kitchen in a grand procession, escorted by forty-eight gentlemen, with the twelve most senior members bearing silver-gilt batons of office. The procession was led from the kitchen building, located across the road from the palace, and wended its way through the many halls and corridors of Versailles before finally reaching Louis, who often dined in his bedroom.[6] As a result, virtually all the food arrived at the king's table tepid, if not stone cold.

Typically, Louis enjoyed six courses at dinner and supper: soup, hors d'oeuvre, entrée, small entrée, roast, and dessert. An entrée could consist of an entire roasted veal rump; a small entrée might be a baked meat pie or grilled fowl. During Lent, fish replaced meat dishes, and the king adopted a penitential diet that included oysters, perch, pike, sole, and salmon. Louis had a hearty appetite, as attested by the Palatine Princess, who described a typical royal meal: "I have very often seen the king eat four plates of different soups, an entire pheasant, a partridge, a large plateful of salad, mutton cut up in its juice with garlic, two good pieces of ham, a plateful of cakes and fruits and jams." If the king felt peckish during the night, at his door he would find a bottle of mineral water, two bottles of wine, and freshly baked dinner rolls.

The interest in fine food among the French upper class was not limited to its consumption. Louis XV, Louis XIV's great-grandson, liked to whip up his favorite foods in the kitchens of Versailles. His signature dish was chicken with basil. One of his generals, Charles, Prince de Soubise, was also an accomplished cook, renowned for his rich pheasant-and-partridge-eggs omelet and a dish known as *purée Soubise*, a kind of risotto made with onion, butter, and rice and served as a sauce with roasted meat.

But not even the wealthiest aristocrats and churchmen, let alone the bourgeoisie, were able to re-create the sumptuous meals of Versailles. The result was a reaction against the culinary excesses of the court and the development of a cuisine that was refined but accessible to all but the king's most impoverished subjects.

François Marin, author of the cookbook *Les Dons de Comus* (The Gifts of Comus [the Roman god of revelry]), wrote in 1739 of this "nouvelle cuisine" that had succeeded the over-the-top gastronomic feats in the court of Louis XIV. "Modern cuisine," he wrote, "established on the foundations of the old one, with less pomp and impediment, although with just as much variety, is simpler and perhaps more complex." Marin assured his middle-class readers that the aristocracy did not have a monopoly on fine dining. The trick, he said, was to shop daily for the freshest ingredients, to employ a cook who could make a superior bouillon, and to furnish one's kitchen with the proper pots, pans, and utensils to ensure successful preparation.

In spite of the bourgeoisie's interest in fine food at a sensible level, extravagant royal menus were still being served during the reign of Louis XVI and Marie Antoinette, when Jefferson arrived in Paris. The philosopher Jean-Jacques Rousseau called for a cuisine even simpler than that advocated by Marin. He urged his readers to give up meat, which he claimed made humankind barbarous, and to dine on milk, eggs, and fresh vegetables. Jefferson, an avid reader of Rousseau, adopted the philosopher's dietary guidelines. Looking back on a lifetime of eating habits, Jefferson declared in 1819: "I have lived temperately, eating little animal food [i.e., meat], and that . . . as a condiment for the vegetables, which constitute my principal diet."

Of course, Rousseau's vegetarian diet appealed to only a tiny portion of French society, but his call for an uncomplicated cuisine resonated widely. Women of the bourgeoisie had already modified the fussy recipes of the court chefs to create dishes that were delicious and refined, yet relatively easy to prepare. This was the style of French cooking that Jefferson would enjoy during his two-year stay in Paris and that James Hemings would study as an apprentice. It was also the forerunner of the French cooking that Julia Child mastered in the 1950s and brought to American home cooks in the 1960s.

It is the rare ambassador, consul, or commerce commissioner who does not travel overseas and return home with some remembrance of service abroad. Still, Jefferson was no souvenir hunter. America was young, raw, and unsophisticated. Whatever was best in Europe, he wanted for his own nation—and that included foodstuffs, recipes, and kitchen utensils. Together with James Hemings, his trusted slave, Jefferson set out to transform America's palate.

Chapter 1

AMERICANS IN PARIS

Twelve-year-old Patsy Jefferson was dreadfully seasick. Although summer was the best season for an Atlantic crossing and the sea had been, as she described, "smooth as a river," the movement of the brand-new brig *Ceres* made her violently ill. While her father enjoyed the days at sea, chatting with the ship's owner, Nathaniel Tracy, and observing whales and sharks, Patsy spent her days lying in her bunk below deck, rising only to vomit into a bucket.

Jefferson was a man who could never be idle, and so when he was not making polite conversation with Tracy, he spent several hours every day teaching himself Spanish from a grammar book and a copy of Miguel Cervantes's novel *Don Quixote*. He would later tell John Quincy Adams that Spanish was such a simple language, he had mastered it in a matter of days. Young Adams was dubious. As he confided to his diary:

"Mr. Jefferson tells large stories."

Jefferson welcomed his appointment as the third American commerce commissioner in France. Only two years earlier his beloved wife, Martha, had died after giving birth to their sixth child, Lucy Elizabeth. Jefferson was overwhelmed by grief. For three weeks, he refused to leave his room. When he finally emerged, he went on long rides into the forest, with Patsy—then ten years old—as his only companion. She would recall later, "On those melancholy rambles I was . . . a solitary witness to many a violent burst of grief."[1] A few years overseas would provide Jefferson with a welcome escape from memory-haunted Monticello.

But the Continent would offer more than just a distraction from grief. In addition to securing import commercial relationships for American businesses, Jefferson knew that Europe possessed scientific instruments and useful household devices unavailable in the United States. He was determined to seek out and bring home any advancements that would improve life in rude, rough-hewn America.

Only four days after Congress confirmed Jefferson's appointment as commerce minister to France (an honor he would share with Benjamin Franklin and John Adams), he set out for Philadelphia, where Patsy was attending school. Jefferson had decided to take his eldest daughter to France. His younger children, six-year-old Mary and two-year-old Lucy, were too young to make a voyage across the Atlantic, so he sent them to live with their aunt and uncle, Elizabeth and Francis Eppes, in Eppington, Virginia.

It took the Jeffersons and James a month to travel from Philadelphia to Boston. They took their time, journeying through New Jersey, New York (where they spent a week in New York City), Connecticut, and Rhode Island before finally arriving in Boston on June 18.[2] Just before midnight on the Fourth of July, the group boarded the *Ceres* bound for England. About five the next morning the ship set sail, and on July 26 it docked at the seaport town of West Cowes. Being on solid ground again was a relief to Patsy, but it took time for her to recover fully. Jefferson rented rooms at an inn in nearby Portsmouth so that his daughter could rest and regain her strength. Dr. Thomas Meik, the physician of the Portsmouth garrison, examined the girl, prescribed medication, and sent a nurse; according to Jefferson's account book, he paid the nurse $2.00 and the apothecary $2.06.[3] On July 30, Patsy was well enough to make the last leg of the journey—another sea voyage, this time across the English Channel to Le Havre.[4] A violent storm accompanied by torrential rain made the crossing an ordeal for poor Patsy. Once again sick and miserable, she lay down fully dressed on a bunk that she said was more like a box than a bed and tried to sleep.

Immediately upon arriving in France, more troubles ensued. Although Patsy had learned to read French, she could not speak the language and found herself unable to put together a single coherent sentence. Jefferson fared not much better. He had studied French as a young man, but his tutor was a Presbyterian minister with a Scots burr so thick that it mangled proper pronunciation. When Jefferson spoke what he believed to be French, no one could understand him. Fortunately, an Irishman was at the dock and, seeing the Jeffersons' predicament, stepped in, spoke to the porters, and escorted the Americans to an inn where he arranged for their rooms.[5]

Adding to Jefferson's embarrassment, he suspected that the porters were cheating him yet said nothing because, as a Virginia gentleman, he was unable to bring himself to haggle. And then there were the beggars. Jefferson had brought along his phaeton, a four-wheeled two-passenger carriage drawn by two horses, which was driven by James. The Americans' stylish carriage and well-tailored clothing marked them as well-to-do, so that everywhere they stopped they were surrounded by a pathetic crowd of the hungry and the homeless. Neither Jefferson nor Patsy had seen so many destitute people clamoring for coins, and the sight shocked them. Yet Jefferson dispensed coins every day—a total of six livres and seven sous, about half what it cost him for meals and a night's lodging for himself, Patsy, and James.[6]

Although the American travelers found the swarms of beggars appalling, the French countryside delighted father and daughter alike. Virginia was still largely wilderness, so France seemed to the Jeffersons to be one grand, well-tended garden. "Nothing," Jefferson wrote to James Monroe, "could be more fertile, better cultivated, or more elaborately improved."[7] Patsy was especially taken with the Gothic churches. There were no churches of such size or so richly adorned in America. The soaring arches, sublime altars, the sculptures, paintings, and gold and silver ornaments were unlike anything she had ever experienced in the austere Protestant churches back home. The stained-glass windows in particular enchanted her—they were probably the first she had ever seen.[8]

On August 6, 1784, after five days on the road, the Jeffersons and James reached Paris. The first thing they would have seen was the new wall surrounding the city, ten feet tall and eighteen miles in circumference. The old massive walls that had protected Paris during the Middle Ages were long gone; the new ones were designed not to fortify the city but to improve its finances. The French government was strapped for cash, a situation made worse by the $40 million that Louis XVI had spent on the American Revolution. Without the medieval ramparts, farmers, tradespeople, and merchants were able to enter and leave the city freely, skirting the tollhouses where they were supposed to pay municipal customs duties. The government could not afford to lose so much revenue, and so it erected a new barrier.

The plan was the brainchild of Antoine Lavoisier, marquis de Condorcet (best remembered today as the chemist who discovered that water is composed of two parts hydrogen and one part oxygen). In the 1780s, Lavoisier was a senior partner in

France's tax-collecting system. Historian Simon Schama notes that the marquis embodied the contradictions of Louis XVI's France. "Lavoisier," Schama writes, "was at once pioneering and arcane, intellectually free and institutionally captive, public-spirited but employed by the most notoriously self-interested private corporation."[9] In spite of his scientific credentials, Lavoisier allied himself with the government's tax police, an army twenty thousand strong whose task it was to ensure that every citizen paid every sou owed to the crown. The result was not only an explosion in smuggling but also the birth of yet another reason to loathe the government of the king.

The wall was designed and erected by the architect Claude-Nicolas Ledoux (1736–1806). It featured forty-seven gates accompanied by forty-seven tollhouses, all designed in the style of neoclassical temples. In these tollhouses, the customs duties were scrupulously collected.[10] Not surprisingly, the wall provoked a storm of protest. When the French Revolution erupted in 1789, both it and the tollhouses were among the targets of the Paris mob.

To enter Paris, the Jeffersons and James rolled across the Bridge of Neuilly, through the Neuilly gate, and then onto the Champs-Elysées. Most Americans in the French capital frequented the Hôtel d'Orléans, and Jefferson directed James to find it. What none among them knew was that the city had two establishments with this name, and Jefferson and his traveling party went to the wrong one.

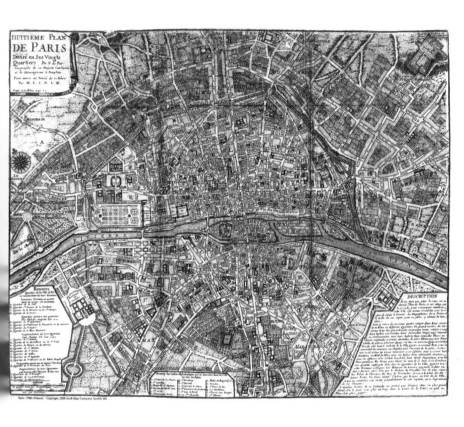

Paris in the 1700s. This map shows the wall surrounding the city center. The Hôtel d'Orléans on the Left Bank was on rue des Petits-Augustins (present-day rue Bonaparte). Jefferson's later primary residence, the Hôtel de Langeac, was at the corner of the rue de Berri and the Champs-Elysées.

Jefferson could be excused for such an error: the Hôtel d'Orléans where he rented rooms stood on rue de Richelieu beside the Palais-Royal, a palace owned by the Duke of Orléans, a cousin of Louis XVI. The duke, who dabbled in real-estate speculation, had hired an architect to transform the structure and surrounding area into a combination pleasure garden, restaurant district, and shopping mall. It became one of the most fashionable and popular spots in Paris. Indeed, the author and playwright Sébastien Mercier (1740–1814) proclaimed the Palais-Royal "the capital of Paris," for "there you can see everything, hear everything, learn everything." Obviously, the city's social center would attract newcomers like the Jeffersons. But for all the excitement of the neighborhood, they missed the company of other Americans, and so, on August 10, they moved to the other Hôtel d'Orléans, located on the Left Bank.

Jefferson quickly realized that he lacked the wardrobe suitable for a representative of a foreign government. He may have looked like an aristocrat back in Virginia, but among the French elites, dressed in their silk, brocade, and velvet suits, their silver and gold trimmed ruffs, their powdered wigs, and their jewel-encrusted swords, Jefferson looked like a country bumpkin. To make himself more presentable, he purchased a sword, shoe buckles, and lace ruffles for his coats and ordered suits made in the French manner. He also called in a dressmaker, a milliner, and a shoemaker to fashion an entirely new set of clothes and accessories for Patsy.[11]

Jefferson's fellow commissioners in Paris were Benjamin Franklin and John Adams. At forty-one, Jefferson was the youngest of the three—Adams was forty-nine years old, and Franklin was seventy-eight. The men had come to know one another well in Philadelphia in the summer of 1776, when they were part of the committee appointed by the Continental Congress to write a document explaining to the world the American colonies' reasons for severing ties with England. There were in fact five men on that committee—the other two were Roger Sherman of Connecticut and Robert Livingston of New York—but when Jefferson had completed his draft of his Declaration of Independence, he showed it only to Franklin and Adams, asking for their suggestions.

Theirs was in many ways an unusual friendship. Jefferson was a member of the Virginia aristocracy and a graduate of the College of William and Mary. Like Adams, he was a lawyer and a farmer, but Jefferson was also a slave owner. He tended to be reserved, whereas Adams, who came from Massachusetts Puritan stock and had been Harvard educated, was outspoken and, by temperament, irascible, cranky, and opinionated. Adams feared that when the history of America's struggle for independence was written, his contributions would be overshadowed by George Washington's exploits on the battlefield, Jefferson's Declaration of Independence, and Franklin's diplomatic successes in France.

And then there was Franklin, a self-made man without a

college education who, in his teens, had run away from his parents' home in Boston to make a new life for himself in Philadelphia. He was a writer, newspaper publisher, printer, postmaster, amateur scientist, and inventor whose creations included the lightning rod, a wood-burning stove, and bifocals. He was also the most amiable of the three. It was thanks to his charm offensive in Paris that France agreed to ally itself with the fledgling United States, virtually guaranteeing an American victory over the British. Franklin had arrived in France in 1776, only months after the Continental Congress adopted the Declaration of Independence. At first, he was America's unofficial envoy, but once France had sided with America in its revolution, he became a full-fledged ambassador, or minister plenipotentiary, as the post was known at the time.

Franklin had traveled to France determined to be a celebrity. Dressed in a brown homespun suit rather than the silk that was de rigueur among the aristocracy, and sporting a fur cap on his bald head instead of a powdered wig, the American portrayed himself as a simple, honest, down-to-earth Quaker rustic who was amiable and direct when speaking to prince or peasant. From top to bottom, French society was enchanted by the affable Dr. Franklin. He was invited to dinners and salons where the country's most powerful, most influential men and women gathered. In such crowds Franklin could be witty and flirtatious, but he was never frivolous. In the late 1770s, America needed a military alliance with France, and it was Franklin who secured it. And when in the early 1780s America needed a trade partner, it was Franklin who opened French markets to American goods. He understood that among the proper crowd, the chatter around a dinner table and within a drawing room could be the first step toward forging favorable political alliances or trade agreements. As he confided in his journal: "Great Affairs sometimes take their Rise from small Circumstances."[12]

Adams was not charmed by Franklin's diplomatic charade. He complained that Franklin's "name was familiar to government and people. To foreign courtiers, nobility, clergy and philosophers, as well as plebeians, to such a degree there was scarcely a peasant or a citizen, a valet de chambre, coachman or footman, a lady's chamber maid or a scullion in a kitchen . . . who did not consider him as a friend. . . . When they spoke of him, they seemed to think he was to restore the golden age." Thanks to Adams's grousing and griping, we have a marvelously detailed portrait of Franklin's life in Paris. When not entertaining at home, Franklin dined out, returning in the small hours of the morning. As a result, he slept late, frustrating Adams's desire to discuss diplomatic business before breakfast. The morning meal was barely concluded when the first callers appeared at Franklin's door. Adams writes of a "crowd of carriages" rolling up to the house, bearing "philosophers, academicians and economists . . . but by far the greater part were women and children come to have the honor to see the great

Franklin and to have the pleasure of telling stories about his simplicity, his balding head and scattering straight hairs."

Initially, Franklin brought Adams along to the dinner parties and salons at the homes of individuals who stood at the pinnacle of French society. There, amid the superb meals, the sparkling Champagne, and the even more sparkling wit, Franklin set about launching a subtle public relations campaign to make the newly formed United States of America a cause célèbre among the French elites. But Adams couldn't see it. He detested these soirées with Franklin, dismissing them as "dissipations [that] were not the objects of my mission to France."

As the inventor of the lightning rod, Franklin was regarded by the French as a kind of demigod who had unlocked the secret of controlling nature's power. It was just one more thing to gall Adams. But there were more to come. Writing in his diary on April 29, 1778, Adams recorded that he and Franklin had attended a gathering at the Academy of Sciences; also present that evening was Voltaire. The audience began to clamor for the two great men to be introduced to each other. Standing before the assembly, the gentlemen shook hands, but that was not enough. Someone shouted, "Let them embrace, in the French manner!" The crowd took up the cry, and so, as Adams describes it, "the two Aged Actors upon this great Theatre of Philosophy and frivolity then embraced each other by hugging one another in their Arms and kissing each other's cheeks, and the tumult subsided." Adams imagined that accounts of the scene would spread throughout France and across Europe, and he always described it in the same way: "How charming it was! Oh it was enchanting to see Solon and Sophocles embracing!"[13] Even worse was Franklin's conduct toward French women. It appears that he kissed almost every one he met—a form of greeting that was perfectly natural in France but made straight-laced Americans suspect the elderly Franklin of sexual dalliance on an impressive scale. Indeed, another American in Paris, Arthur Lee of Virginia, wrote to his brother Richard Henry Lee that Franklin had become a "wicked old man ... [wallowing in a] corrupt hotbed of vice."[14]

Adams's bitterness did not escape Jefferson's notice. In a letter to James Madison, he wrote: "[Adams] hates Franklin, he hates Jay, he hates the French, he hates the English. To whom will he adhere?" Nor was Franklin oblivious to his colleague's resentments. At one point, he claimed that Adams was "sometimes, and in some things, out of his senses."

Yet despite the clash of personalities, one thing remained unchanged: Adams and Franklin maintained a fundamental respect for each other as intelligent men striving to advance the interests of their country in a world hostile to the ideas of liberty and human rights.[15] And, in spite of all the carping from his fellow commissioner, Franklin knew what he was doing. His charismatic approach to diplomacy secured for the politically shaky, cash-strapped United States $40 million in loans and outright gifts from the government of Louis XVI.

Once in Paris, Franklin was the first person Jefferson called upon. Doing so required a thirty-minute carriage ride out to the suburbs to a lovely place called Passy, a collection of pretty villas overlooking the Seine and surrounded by the Bois de Boulogne. At Passy, Franklin was far from the dirt, noise, smells, and crowds of Paris but still close to Versailles, the center of French political power. The day the Jeffersons stepped into Franklin's house, the statesman was seventy-eight years old. He suffered from bladder stones, a condition that became almost unbearable whenever he was compelled to make a carriage ride over the rough country roads and unevenly paved streets of Paris. And so Franklin spent most of his days at home, where he received a constant stream of visitors.

Franklin's residence, the Hôtel de Valentinois, was built early in the eighteenth century by the duke of Valentinois, who situated it upon a hill overlooking the Seine and the skyline of Paris. Although we know nothing about the appearance of its interior, we do know that the home had spacious terraced gardens planted with chestnut and fruit trees, flower beds, and fountains, the whole surrounded by eighteen acres of woods.[16] Franklin added his own distinguishing mark to the structure by installing a lightning rod on the roof.

If Franklin was fond of Jefferson, Jefferson genuinely revered Franklin. He once wrote that Franklin was "the greatest man and ornament of the age." Of Franklin's embassy to the French court, Jefferson wrote: "More respect and veneration attached to the character of Dr. Franklin in France than to that of any other person, foreign or native."[17]

Adams, too, preferred to live outside Paris. He had always been a firm believer in the benefits of fresh country air, an opinion confirmed in his own mind after he fell seriously ill, first in Amsterdam and then in Paris.[18] He rented a house—the Hôtel de Ruhault—in Auteuil, which, like Passy, was a hilltop village overlooking the Seine and surrounded by the Bois de Boulogne. Adams was not a man who gave free rein to enthusiasm, but, on the day he moved into the house, he let himself go: "The house, the garden, the situation near the Bois de Boulogne, elevated above the river Seine and the low grounds, and distant from the putrid streets of Paris, is the best I could wish for."

Adams had traveled to France in 1778 with his eldest son, eleven-year-old John Quincy. Now, in 1784, as Jefferson arrived in Paris, Adams's wife, Abigail, and their eldest daughter, nineteen-year-old Abigail (called Nabby by the family), were joining him at Auteuil. The presence of his wife and two of his children lifted Adams's spirits, as revealed in a letter he wrote to Arthur Lee: "I feel more at home than I have ever done in Europe." The Auteuil mansion featured either forty or fifty rooms (depending upon which source one consults), complete with a private theater. Parts of the residence were in a sad state, including the dilapidated theater, which would need considerable renovation before any plays could be staged there, if ever the Adamses found themselves in the mood to do so.

For Abigail Adams, who had raised five children in a seven-room farmhouse in Massachusetts, the house at Auteuil was overwhelming, perhaps almost intimidating. The family occupied the second floor, where every room had at least one pair of French doors that opened onto the gardens and grounds. The walls of one octagonal chamber were covered, floor to ceiling, with enormous mirrors. Of all the rooms in the house, this one Abigail made a point of avoiding. In a letter to her niece Betsy Cranch, she said of it: "I do not like [the mirror room], for being rather clumsy, and by no means an elegant figure, I hate to have it repeated to me."[19]

Then there was the matter of domestic help. Adams's salary was $9,000—a generous sum back in Massachusetts but entirely inadequate in Paris, where everything was expensive. The family could afford to hire only seven servants, which underscored to the diplomatic community the poverty of the newly independent United States, given that the ambassador from England had fifty servants and the ambassador from Spain, seventy-five.[20] Nevertheless, the gardens and grounds delighted the family. Flowers flourished in large pots, and there were fruit trees, including orange trees (oranges were a rare delicacy in America). Even the broken fountain and the tumbled-down summerhouse charmed Abigail.

In Paris, Jefferson became close friends with the Adamses, especially Abigail, who said that her newfound friend was "one of the choice ones of the earth."[21] As for Jefferson, ever the inveterate shopper, he introduced Abigail and Nabby to the finery of Paris. The Hermits of Mount Calvary, a religious order, supported themselves by making silk stockings; Jefferson recommended the product to the ladies, who were instantly delighted by his choice. After the Adamses left France for England, Abigail wrote often to Jefferson, sending him shopping lists of items unavailable there, such as certain types of dessert plates or the silk stockings that she and Nabby now could not live without.[22]

*　　*　　*

In the eighteenth century Southerners routinely referred to their enslaved servants and farmworkers as members of the family. In the case of James Hemings and Thomas Jefferson, the familial connection was literal rather than figurative. About 1761, John Wayles, a thrice-widowed lawyer and plantation owner who would eventually become Jefferson's father-in-law, took Elizabeth Hemings as his concubine. Hemings was one of the house slaves at the Forest, the Wayles family's plantation. She was about twenty-six years old when the affair with her master began; he was about forty-six. Over the next dozen years, they would have six children together, three boys and three girls. James, who was born in 1765, was Elizabeth and John's second child.[23] Wayles also had four white children, all girls; the eldest, Martha, became the wife of Thomas Jefferson in 1772.

On the death of John Wayles in 1773, Jefferson inherited his father-in-law's property, slaves, and considerable debts, which amounted to £4,000.[24] Because Wayles had made no provision in his will for the emancipation of Elizabeth Hemings and his children borne by her, the enslaved family was transferred to Monticello. The six Hemings children were Martha Wayles's half-siblings and, therefore, Jefferson's in-laws, although that relationship was not recognized by law. To hold members of one's own family as slaves may sound shocking, but such arrangements were common at the time.

There may have been a family resemblance between Martha and the Hemings children as well. As Mary Boykin Chesnut, the renowned Civil War–era Southern diarist, wrote in 1861: "Like the patriarchs of old, our men live all in one house with their wives & their concubines, & the Mulattos one sees in every family exactly resemble the white children & every lady tells you who is the father of all the Mulatto children in everybody's household, but those in her own, she seems to think drop from the clouds or pretends so to think."[25]

At the time of his father-in-law's death, Jefferson owned fifty-two slaves. From Wayles he inherited another 135, making him the second largest slave owner in Virginia's Albemarle County. For the rest of his life, at any given moment Jefferson owned about two hundred slaves. He was never an active slave trader; when he bought an enslaved person, it was usually to fulfill a need in his house or on one of his farms. He also sometimes bought slaves for compassionate reasons: to unite a husband and wife, for example (even though marriage between slaves was not recognized under Virginia law).[26] His own precarious finances often required him to sell his slaves. Lucy Stanton, senior research historian at Monticello, has found that between 1784 and 1794, Jefferson sold or gave as gifts 161 enslaved members of his household.[27]

Jefferson's views on slavery were inconsistent. On one hand, he condemned the institution as an "abominable crime," a "moral depravity," a "hideous blot" that was an offense against natural law. On the other hand, he relied on enslaved labor all his life; indeed, when one of his slaves ran off, he advertised a reward for the man's return. Unlike some other slave owners, such as George Washington, Jefferson did not emancipate his slaves in his will.[28] He recognized his own ambivalence on the subject. On July 18, 1824, toward the end of his life, he wrote: "I am not apt to despair; yet I see not how we are to disengage ourselves from that deplorable entanglement, we have the wolf by the ears and feel the danger of either holding or letting him loose."[29]

That is how an enslaved member of Jefferson's own extended family accompanied him to France. Once settled in Paris, Jefferson put his plans into action. After making inquiries, he apprenticed James Hemings to a restaurateur named

Combeaux, who also operated a catering business. Jefferson paid Combeaux 150 francs to teach James the art of French cuisine. The specifics of the training are unknown, but based on similar arrangements at the time, we can assume that James spent the majority of the week working in Combeaux's kitchen. (Because Hemings was also obligated to perform tasks for Jefferson, he probably did not work with the chef seven days a week.) The apprenticeship marked the beginning of a new life for James Hemings—one that would ultimately lead to his freedom.

Chapter 2

A FREE CITY

J ames Hemings spoke French better than his master. He had no choice: as an apprentice in Combeaux's kitchen, he was surrounded by men who communicated only in French. Perhaps the chef and a few members of his kitchen staff knew a word or two of English, but such limited vocabulary would not have been enough to instruct James in the basics of cooking. And so James would learn the language through immersion.

He got off to a shaky start. In a letter sent to Elizabeth Hemings (James's mother) back at Monticello, Jefferson wrote: "James is well. He has forgot how to speak English, and has not learnt to speak French."[1] Jefferson was being facetious, of course. In fact, James would become a fluent French speaker, just as Jefferson's daughters would. As for Jefferson, although eventually he read the language fluently, he never spoke it well or learned to write it. To save himself from the embarrassment of mangling his speech among French ladies and gentlemen in his social circle, Jefferson sought out the company of Americans and visited salons where all the visitors spoke English in addition to their native tongues. As a result, America's ambassador to France was never comfortable conversing in French, whereas his slave came to be perfectly at ease in the language.[2]

Once the Jeffersons and James Hemings had located the correct Hôtel d'Orléans on the Left Bank, they spent several weeks in the establishment. One of Jefferson's first purchases was eighteen dozen bottles of Bordeaux wine, which he stored in their rooms. He hired a valet de chambre as his personal servant and began looking about for a school for Patsy.[3] Fortunately, he had a friend to advise him. Also living in Paris at the time was François-Jean de Beauvoir, the marquis de Chastellux. In 1779 Chastellux was one of three major generals under General Rochambeau who commanded the French troops sent by Louis XVI to America in support of the revolution. Chastellux was fluent in English, and during the winter months, when armies typically did not fight, he would travel around the colonies, calling upon some of the country's most distinguished men: Samuel Adams, James Madison, and, of course, Thomas Jefferson.

Chastellux visited Jefferson at Monticello and found himself enchanted by the beautiful house that Jefferson had designed for himself. He would later write: "Mr. Jefferson is the first American who has consulted the Fine Arts to know how he should shelter himself from the weather." But Chastellux's initial impression of his host was not so enthusiastic. "I found [Mr. Jefferson's] first appearance serious, nay, even cold." Jefferson's reticence with the stranger did not last. "Before I had been two hours with him," Chastellux wrote, "we were as intimate as if we had passed our whole lives together." The two new friends sat up nights discussing architecture and literature. When Jefferson discovered Chastellux's interest in geology, he organized an excursion to the Natural Bridge, one of Virginia's most striking landmarks.[4]

When Jefferson arrived in Paris, Chastellux was one of only two Frenchmen he knew (the other was the Marquis de Lafayette). It was Chastellux who suggested that Jefferson send Patsy to the Abbaye Royale de Panthemont in the Faubourg Saint-Germain. The Abbaye de Panthemont was one of the most selective schools in Paris, its student body restricted to the daughters of nobility or other distinguished families. As the child of an American diplomat, Patsy probably would not have been turned away. Nevertheless, Chastellux wrote a letter of recommendation to the abbess, Madame Béthisy de Mézières. Madame l'Abbesse, as she was called, was half Scottish, being descended on her mother's side from the Sutton d'Oglethorpe family, who had supported Bonnie Prince Charlie in his attempt to claim the crown of England and Scotland. She had reigned over the abbey and the school since 1743.

Patsy was enrolled at the Abbaye de Panthemont in 1785; at the time, about fifty or sixty girls were in residence. Also there at the same time as Patsy was Joséphine de Beauharnais, the future lover, wife, and empress of Napoleon Bonaparte;[5] in addition to operating a school for girls, the nuns also offered rooms to aristocratic ladies who sought a quiet retreat from their troubles, whether the lack of a husband, the death of a husband, or the separation from a husband. The girls' uniform was a crimson frock. They studied arithmetic, geography, and history as well as drawing, needlework, music, and dancing. Patsy learned to play the harpsichord from Claude Balbastre, the organist at the Cathedral of Notre-Dame. She wrote to a friend in America that, upon arriving at the school, "I did not speak a word of French." Her immersion among nuns and teachers and students who spoke only French soon corrected that problem. "Speaking as much as I could with them," Patsy continued, "I learnt the language very soon."[6]

Although the nuns remained within the abbey's walls, the girls were free to venture outside. Escorted by Jefferson's growing number of female friends, including Madame de Lafayette, Patsy attended the opera and visited the gardens of Versailles. She was also invited to attend her father's dinner parties. At her first invitation she wore her scarlet frock, which resulted in a note from her father instructing her to "make it a rule hereafter to come dressed otherwise than in your uniform."

Now that Patsy was settled at the convent and James was

apprenticed to Combeaux the caterer, Jefferson could devote himself to finding a house. In late summer of 1785 he located a place that suited him—the Hôtel de Langeac on the Champs-Elysées, at the corner of rue de Berri. The townhouse had been constructed in 1768 by the Comte de Saint-Florentin for his mistress, the Marquise de Langeac, hence the home's name. It then passed to the marquise's son, the Comte de Langeac, who became Jefferson's landlord. It was a two-story, twenty-four-room structure, with a neoclassical facade and an asymmetrical floor plan that was fashionable at the time and that included a circular entry hall and a large oval bedroom and study; these last two rooms Jefferson took as his own. Behind the house was a large garden, where Jefferson laid out a sizeable plot. He wanted to plant American vegetables, and so he wrote to Colonel Nicholas Lewis requesting seeds for sweet potato, watermelon, and "cantelupe" as well as seeds for the "small ripe corn we call Hominy corn." He also asked Lewis to send him "a dozen or two bacon hams." Even amid the gourmet cuisine of Paris, Jefferson still had a hankering for plantation fare. Eventually, he would add Hochheim and Rudesheim grapevines to his garden so that he could begin learning how to make wine, with an eye to transporting vine cuttings to Monticello and starting a vineyard there.

Just as Jefferson enjoyed varying his French table with American produce, he also looked forward to elevating the cuisine at Monticello with the best food and wines Europe had to offer. To make this dream a reality, he befriended Étienne Parent of Beaune, one of France's foremost wine merchants, who sent Jefferson case after case of fine Burgundies. A Dr. Lambert in Montpelier was Jefferson's source for muscat, and the Comte de Lur-Saluces provided him with Sauternes. And so the cellar of the Hôtel de Langeac began to fill.[7]

"I have at length procured a house in a situation much more pleasing to me than my present," Jefferson wrote to Abigail Adams. "It suits me in every circumstance but the price, being dearer than the one I am now in."[8] Jefferson would pay an annual rent of seventy-five hundred livres. The house was unfurnished, which added to his expenses. He hired servants, purchased horses and carriages that filled the stables, and paid fifty livres per year for the luxury of running water inside the house.[9] He then hired Adrien Petit as maître d'hôtel, the servant who ran the entire household, which involved everything from telling the other servants what to do to managing the household accounts. Jefferson also hired a full-time gardener and a full-time coachman. When James Hemings wasn't apprenticing with Combeaux, he was employed as Jefferson's personal servant.[10]

The Jeffersons found themselves welcomed in France, especially among the upper crust. The French elites believed that an ideal society would be simple, honest, and direct in its interaction, a society in which most inhabitants lived in the countryside rather than in the city, a society that despised rank and class, treated everyone as equals, and loved liberty. The

French believed America to be just such a place. Back in 1777 one starry-eyed nineteen-year-old French aristocrat, the Marquis de Lafayette, had left behind titles, château, and wife to volunteer in America's struggle for independence. Before setting sail he wrote to his wife, Adrienne, that he saw himself as a "defender of that liberty which I worship."[11] Writing of Jefferson almost a century later, Henry Adams would say that, between 1784 and 1789, Jefferson could "breathe with perfect satisfaction . . . the liberal, literary, and scientific air of Paris."[12] The historian Annette Gordon-Reed adds: "For the first time in his life, [Jefferson] lived in a society with a large social cohort whose intelligence, erudition, and accomplishments matched or exceeded his own."[13]

Living in Paris was a unique experience for James, too: for the first time in his life, he was essentially a free man. Back home, all Virginians assumed that any black person they encountered was a slave. However, slavery was unknown in France; more to the point, it was illegal. So Parisians who saw black men or women walking through their city may have thought of them as exotic, but never as slaves.

The French were not abolitionists; the government had limited slavery to the French colonies in the Caribbean, Africa, and Asia. Under this contradictory system, it was perfectly acceptable, from the French government's point of view, for slaves to be auctioned to the highest bidder in the markets of Senegal and then shipped to the Caribbean to labor in the fields in Haiti, as long as such scenes were not to be found in Paris or Marseille or any other French city. Yet the legal and political establishment of prerevolutionary France was wrestling with another issue: What should be done in the case of slaves who were brought into France by their colonial masters? One early solution had been to permit the practice, provided that the owners registered their slaves and made a declaration that the slaves had been brought into the country to receive instruction in the Catholic faith or to learn a trade. In such cases, the slave owner would be permitted to return to the colony with his or her "property" at the conclusion of the religious instruction or apprenticeship.[14] A later law passed in 1777 attempted to bar slave owners from bringing their slaves into France in the first place; under this legislation, the slaves were to be held at a depot at their port of arrival and then returned to the colony from which they came. This law, clearly written with the slave owner in mind, was rarely enforced. The masters disembarked in France and took their slaves wherever they liked.

But all such laws were trumped by an even earlier declaration, the Freedom Principle, which stated that an enslaved person became free the moment he or she arrived in France. The Parlement of Paris, the oldest and most influential court in France, routinely rejected any legislation that attempted to limit the Freedom Principle, and the city's lower courts supported its decisions. Consequently, there was no better place for James Hemings to live than in the French capital.[15] In Paris, a slave was entitled to demand freedom from his or her master; if the master refused to grant it, the slave could petition the court for redress. Some slaves also demanded back wages for services rendered, along with their requests for freedom. Annette Gordon-Reed has found that, in the 1780s, records of the admiralty court, where such petitions were filed, declarations from masters who voluntarily freed their slaves outnumber those from slaves demanding their freedom. And, as Gordon-Reed observes, that does not take into account masters who simply freed their slaves outright without filing a declaration with the court.[16]

The moment James set foot in France, he would have been able to claim his freedom, and Jefferson could have done nothing to stop him. Jefferson wrote of the dilemma to Paul Bentalou, an acquaintance and fellow slave owner who had traveled to Paris and brought along one of his slaves to serve him. "I have made enquiries on the subject of the negro boy you have brought," Jefferson wrote, "and find that the laws of France give him freedom if he claims it, and that it will be difficult, if not impossible, to interrupt the course of the law." Then Jefferson added: "I have known an instance where a person bringing in a slave, and saying nothing about it, has not been disturbed in his possession." The unidentified "person" was Jefferson himself, and there was more to that situation than he let on to Bentalou. With James Hemings going to and from his cooking classes, it would be only a matter of time before he would learn of the "no slaves in France" legislation. To prevent James from running off, Jefferson had made him an offer: if he mastered the art of French cuisine and returned home to Monticello to teach his craft to another slave, then Jefferson would grant his freedom. James accepted the deal.

According to the historian Sue Peabody, France in the late eighteenth century had a population of approximately twenty million, of whom between four thousand and five thousand were black. The city with the largest black population was Paris, in which lived approximately a thousand men, women, and children of African descent.[17] Gordon-Reed explains that blacks were concentrated in the city's best neighborhoods, where they worked as servants in the houses of the aristocracy and the well-to-do. Jefferson's home, the Hôtel de Langeac, stood in the fashionable area known as the Faubourg Saint-Germain, so James would surely have met some of these free blacks while running errands or walking to Combeaux's restaurant for cooking lessons. He would have met even more on evenings when Jefferson held dinner parties, for the black servants would have been part of the entourage of Jefferson's distinguished guests.

While in Paris, Jefferson paid James a monthly salary. Furthermore, when James had spare time, he was free to wander about the city at will. In allowing this liberty, Jefferson may have combined generosity with prudence—had he tried to restrict James's mobility, the servant might have run off to the admiralty court (the court charged with enforcing the Freedom Principle) and demanded his emancipation.

No surviving document from Jefferson's years in France records James's impressions, but Paris must have dazzled him. In Virginia, Jefferson was an aristocrat, and his house was considered very fine; the cities James had seen thus far—Philadelphia, New York, Boston—were the pride of the United States. But America's finest cities paled in comparison to Paris, where nobles dwelt in true palaces of dozens of rooms, rattled over cobblestones in gilded carriages, and strode through the halls of Versailles with bejeweled swords swinging by their sides. In Paris, the still-incomplete Monticello would have been mistaken as an outbuilding of a grand estate. With its population of one million, the city could have easily absorbed America's most populous urban centers of Philadelphia, New York, and Boston, with plenty of room to swallow up Providence, Newport, Baltimore, Charleston, and Savannah as well.

In addition to freedom of movement, James had his own money. In Paris in 1785, a servant in a well-off household could expect an annual salary of between one hundred and one hundred fifty livres. Jefferson paid James two hundred eighty-eight livres per year. Once again, perhaps he was generous so that James would not be tempted to claim his freedom. Yet Jefferson was generous to all his household staff in Paris, including his white French servants. Furthermore, unlike Parisian employers who paid their domestic help in one lump sum at the conclusion of a servant's contracted term of service, Jefferson paid his servants once a month.[18]

Jefferson's generosity meant that the servants he employed were fortunate, but it did not alter their status. France, or at least the city of Paris, may have been willing to grant to people such as James the dramatic shift from slave to freeman; yet, in other respects the French social hierarchy remained fixed and rigid. A tradesman could become wealthy, but he would always be a tradesman, never a nobleman. Individuals of lower rank—whether skilled members of the working classes or prosperous merchants—took pride in the quality of their work and guarded their personal respectability, which would earn them the esteem of those both above and below them on the social ladder. The Abbé Grivel, who operated a school in the Faubourg Saint-Antoine, summed it up neatly in his instructions for composing letters to various members of society: "The letters one addresses to one's superiors must always be very respectful; those one addresses to one's equals should be honest and always convey marks of consideration and respect. As for those one writes to one's inferiors, one should always give them evidence of affection and kindness."[19]

Rank and status in late-eighteenth-century France were reflected in dress. The aristocracy, both men and women, wore the most expensive fabrics—cloth of gold and silver, furs, silk, velvet—elaborate wigs, and exquisite jewelry. The middle classes prided themselves on the quality and tailoring of their modest clothing. Lawyers dressed in black or other somber colors to reflect the seriousness of their profession. Laborers wore long aprons that hung from the shoulders to below the knees in an effort to keep their less costly clothes clean. Of course, human nature being what it is, plenty of people in France, and in Paris in particular, dressed in a way that suggested they were of higher rank than they actually were. The desire to rise in status via clothing and accessories could be curbed by members of one's class, who might mock the social climber. If derision failed, there was always the police, who were authorized to arrest a non-noble person for wearing a sword. By the 1780s these old strictures had begun to chafe, especially among professionals such as attorneys and physicians, who were eager to rise above the position assigned to them since the Middle Ages. Surgeons, for example, were especially active in trying to sever their centuries-old ties to barbers and having their calling recognized as a distinct and respectable profession.[20]

In the Paris that James was exploring, scarcely a trace of the old city remained, aside from the churches, the fortresses, and the prisons. Early in the seventeenth century, the city officials had the last medieval houses torn down. Narrow alleys were widened into proper streets, which brought light and fresh air into residential and shopping districts that before had been dark and stifling. A new law mandated that all new streets had to be at least thirty-two feet wide. And beginning in 1667, street lamps were installed, lighting the way for pedestrians and passengers on evening business.[21]

There were other improvements as well. A local politician named Jean-Jacques Renouard de Villayer invented the city's first postal system and erected mailboxes in the best parts of town where the well-to-do could drop their letters and messages for collection and delivery by new postal workers. (In the poorer areas, citizens still delivered their messages the old-fashioned way—in person.) Another entrepreneur was Nicolas Sauvage, a carpenter, who in about 1654 designed and built a carriage called a *carrosse*, which could accommodate several travelers at once. Sauvage's hired coaches became Paris's first public transportation system. Within a decade, twenty such carriages were lined up outside the Hotel St. Fiacre, waiting for passengers. The vehicle soon became known as a fiacre, after the location of its first use.[22]

Urban planning in general was undergoing significant changes. During the Middle Ages, Parisians had built tall houses, piling one floor upon another, a construction style that blocked the sun and plunged a street into perpetual shadow. But in the seventeenth century, as the last medieval houses were being demolished, a new style was introduced: horizontal buildings only two or three stories high, set along the sides of a grand, open square or a broad boulevard. The boulevards were also a new idea; Paris had never before had pedestrian thoroughfares, and they gave rise to a popular trend: walking.

The well-born and the well-heeled took to strolling along the boulevards and around the most popular squares to show off their latest fashions. Borrowing a term from their Norman cousins, Parisians adopted the word *flâner*, meaning "to wander aimlessly."[23]

New construction in the city continued well into the eighteenth century, and at its heart was an enormous square, the Place Louis XV. In the middle of the square stood a giant equestrian statue of the late king dressed as a Roman emperor. Installation of the monument had not been easy. The cart bearing the statue had gotten stuck outside, of all places, the Élysée Palace, which had served as the residence of Louis's mistress, Madame de Pompadour. Once the square had been formally inaugurated, it became one of the most fashionable areas in the city, sparking a residential building boom in the neighborhood and along the nearby rue Saint-Honoré. During the French Revolution, the king's statue was destroyed and a guillotine erected in its place. There Louis XVI and his queen, Marie Antoinette, along with hundreds of lesser French citizens, lost their heads. In 1795, in the aftermath of the Reign of Terror, the square was rechristened as the Place de la Concorde.[24]

Of course, there was more to Paris than palaces and grand boulevards. Like any visitor to the city, then and now, James would have been drawn to the taverns and cafés that are still among the most popular gathering spots. For example, the Pomme de Pin (Pinecone), on rue de la Cité, had been the favorite watering hole of the fifteenth-century poet François Villon. Two hundred years later, Racine and Molière were regular customers there, and it was one of the best-known taverns in the city; it is possible that James patronized it, too.

Cafés or coffeehouses were a relatively new development. Coffee had become a fashionable beverage in the seventeenth century, and it was two Armenian brothers, Pascal and Gregoire Alep, who capitalized on the craze by opening a shop that offered its clientele nothing but the caffeinated beverage.[25] Voltaire stopped by the Café Procope every day, which made the location a hangout for the leaders of the Enlightenment. In the 1780s it was still fashionable with intellectuals, and Jefferson and Franklin were among its customers.

For members of Paris's working class, the city offered pleasure gardens where they could spend a Sunday or a holy day in the company of family and friends, drinking cheap wine, talking, singing, arguing, and perhaps brawling until it was time to stagger home and tumble into bed. Parisians drank alcohol almost exclusively, and they were not alone in their habits; contaminated springs, rivers, streams, and ponds made it unsafe to drink water in the Old World as well as in the New, and so most Europeans and Americans drank beer, ale, hard cider, and wine. Many Parisians began the day not with a cup of coffee, but with a glass of chilled white wine. John Adams had a habit of starting his morning off with a tankard of hard cider. The drinking went on all day long in Paris, where breaks from work for a snack and a few glasses of wine were part of every laborer's routine.[26]

Exactly how much wine French laborers downed during the course of a workday is unknown, but they didn't appear to be drunk to Jefferson. In a letter to a Mr. Bellini dated 1785, he remarked that he admired the sobriety of Parisians and feared for his own countrymen, who were succumbing to "the poison of whiskey, which is destroying them by wholesale."[27] Yet Jefferson's information regarding French drinking habits was inaccurate. On average, a single Parisian drank approximately 155 liters of wine per year. Louis-Sébastien Mercier tells us that on Sundays the city's poor and working people walked to taverns in the suburbs for a day of drinking. According to Mercier, after dark, "regiments of drunks return to town . . . staggering, beating the walls. . . . The drunkenness of the Parisian people is abominable and horrible."[28]

As a culinary apprentice and the servant of an American diplomat, James Hemmings would have spent most of his time in the best parts of town. On his own, however, he may have wandered into working-class neighborhoods, such as the Faubourg Saint-Antoine, where laborers and their families lived in crowded apartment buildings. Such places were teeming with people, but the neighborhoods were more or less safe for strangers. Virtually all the inhabitants earned a living, and local shops and markets were well supplied with food and other goods.

James's acquaintances would have warned him to stay

clear of the city's slums, however. Dark and filthy, populated by the most desperate people, these dangerous areas were shunned by the upper classes and avoided by the working class. Unemployment, disease, and early death were omnipresent in the slums, where a population density of 1,000 to 1,300 people per 2.5 acres was typical.[29] Residents had few job skills; they had never mastered a trade and tended to take temporary work as laborers on construction projects. They were often underemployed, if not altogether unemployed.[30] The unspoken fear among the well-to-do was that a famine or epidemic would drive the slum dwellers to the breaking point and provoke a riot that would sweep across the city. Even the Marquis de Lafayette, whose exploits during the American Revolution had proved he was a friend of liberty and an enemy of tyranny, worried about the potential for violence. Writing to César Maubourg, the comte de la Tour, Lafayette said: "One must not play games with a population as numerous as that of Paris, where the slightest disturbance can go further than people think." Lafayette's fears came to life on July 14, 1789, when an angry mob stormed the Bastille, the first act of violence that, in a matter of six years, would spill an ocean of blood and convulse France in ways Lafayette could not have imagined.[31]

Life in France changed Thomas Jefferson. He is typically remembered as an ardent gardener, a conscientious farmer, and an advocate of the simple life in the country, yet Paris inspired his secret passion—the excitement of urban living. While

Adams and Franklin settled in bucolic suburbs, Jefferson took up residence in the heart of the capital. He bought a street map and took long walks exploring the neighborhoods, studying the new buildings and the old, and recording his opinions of both. Gothic architectural landmarks such as the Cathedral of Notre Dame and the Church of St. Germain des Prés did not touch Jefferson—he considered them relics of the barbarous Middle Ages, when church and state crushed the simple faith of the people beneath the tonnage of hierarchy, ritual, tradition, and incomprehensible doctrines. He favored newer churches built in the neoclassical style, such as St. Philippe du Roule, near his home, and Ste. Geneviève (now Les Invalides), which featured bright, open designs based on the classic architectural styles of ancient Greece and Rome. Jefferson's preference for natural light and fresh air led him to applaud the transformation of the city's oldest bridge, the Pont Neuf. Inaugurated in 1607, the bridge had grown crowded with tiny shops and houses perched along its edges, reducing the passage across the Seine to a dark, constricted alley. In 1787 the shops and houses were torn down and the bridge was restored to its original, grand, unencumbered appearance.[32]

The one thing Paris lacked was the presence of a royal family. Since 1682, when Louis XIV made Versailles the seat of government, the monarch and his family no longer lived in the capital. Although Louis had authorized the refurbishing of the Louvre and Tuileries palaces, he rarely stayed in either, and his successors followed his example. Consequently, Louis XVI, Marie Antoinette, and their children appeared in Paris only for special events. One such exception took place on April 1, 1785. On that occasion Jefferson would experience the soon-to-be-extinguished splendor of the ancient regime. The queen, Marie Antoinette, had given birth to a son, Louis Charles, and to celebrate the birth of the prince, Louis called for a Te Deum to be sung at the Cathedral of Notre Dame. Thanks to the intervention of the Marquis de Lafayette, Jefferson and John Quincy Adams, along with several other Americans in Paris, were invited to the ceremony and given prime seats in a specially constructed gallery overlooking the high altar.

To the American Protestants, the scene at Notre Dame, now decked out for a grand royal occasion, would have been dazzling. Jefferson, who was nominally Episcopalian, would have been familiar with the cadences of the Book of Common Prayer, which, although majestic, were part of church services that were rather austere. Young Adams had been raised in the strict Calvinism of his Puritan ancestors. The Sunday services he had attended would have been even more austere— no prayerbook, no organ music, no vestments for the clergy, and no decoration whatsoever. Both men were impressed by the spectacle they witnessed in the Paris cathedral. In his diary Adams wrote a detailed account of the event, including what the nobles and other dignitaries were wearing and where they were seated, how the king and his two brothers fell to their knees the moment they arrived at their places in the sanctuary, and the quality of the singing of the choir ("exceeding fine music") and of the archbishop of Paris ("his voice seems to be much broken"). According to Adams: "What a charming sight: an absolute king of one of the most powerful Empires on earth, and perhaps a thousand of the first personages in that Empire, adoring the divinity who created them and acknowledging that he can reduce them to the Dust from which they sprung. . . . I was vastly pleased with the Ceremony."[33]

Despite its impressiveness, most likely Jefferson was not vastly pleased with the ceremony. He never cared for pomp and splendor. In fact, years later, on the day he was inaugurated as president of the United States, he *walked* to the Capitol to take the oath of office. Moreover, the throng in Notre Dame that day would not have appealed to him, for he disliked kings, princes, and aristocrats. Even during the Reign of Terror, when the revolutionaries raged out of control, he still preferred republican France, however bloody, over law-abiding but monarchical England.

What did please Jefferson was the city itself. "A walk about Paris," he said, "will provide lessons in history, beauty, and in the point of Life." The historians Lucia Stanton and Douglas L. Wilson believe that the five years Jefferson lived in the French capital were "arguably the most memorable of his life. Paris—with its music, its architecture, its savants and salons, its learning and enlightenment, not to mention its elegant social life . . . had worked its enchantments on this rigidly self-controlled Virginia gentleman."

Paris changed the life of James Hemings as well. It was there that he lived as a free man. And as he learned the art of French cooking, he looked forward to the day when he would return to America and become completely and truly free.

Chapter 3

A FEAST FOR THE PALATE

W riting about the comfortable life enjoyed by the French bourgeoisie, especially those people living in Paris, Voltaire said: "More poultry and game is eaten in Paris in one day than in a week in London. . . . [I]n no other city in the world does a larger number of citizens enjoy so much abundance of all good things."[1]

What Voltaire failed to mention was the daily challenge of feeding a city of one million inhabitants. Twice a week in the mid-eighteenth century, 60,000 cattle, 400,000 sheep, and 125,000 calves, not to mention an unknown number of pigs and goats, were herded into the city's markets. Suburban villages such as Montreuil and Passy were home to massive market gardens where all manner of fruits and vegetables were grown to be sold in the capital, thirty minutes away. The village of Vaugirard was famous for its artificial garden beds in which vast quantities of mushrooms were cultivated. Farms outside Paris provided milk, butter, eggs, and some cheeses, notably those made from goat's milk, although varieties from outlying provinces, such as Gruyère and Roquefort, were also available. Then there was wine, considered indispensable by members of all of France's social classes; it was brought in by the cask via boat from the renowned vineyards of Burgundy and Beaujolais.

Inside the city were institutions and individuals who attempted to supply at least some of their own food. Monasteries and convents, as well as many of the large properties owned by nobles and the well-to-do, were equipped with vegetable and herb gardens, orchards, and even fish ponds. John and Abigail Adams were delighted to find orange trees growing in their garden at Auteuil. Even in the heart of the city, small-scale farming was undertaken by tenants who kept chickens, rabbits, and pigs in their courtyards.

But the essential food—the staple of the French diet—was bread. Sacks of grain and flour arrived almost daily to satisfy Parisians' appetite for fresh loaves. A bad harvest resulting in shortages of grain could result in murderous riots in which the targets of the mob's fury were indiscriminate, from humble bakers to grain speculators to merchants suspected (sometimes correctly) of hoarding supplies of grain and flour in an effort to drive up prices.

All this meat and produce and grain had to be transformed into meals for thousands of hungry citizens, and comprehensive cookbooks soon became widely available to aid in food preparation. The quintessential guide to all things culinary was *Les Dons de Comus*, a three-volume cookbook published in 1739 by François Marin. The chef addressed his book to "the enlightened public," meaning the bourgeoisie, who had come to appreciate fine food. Chefs de cuisine, all of them men, disdained working for the middle classes and held out for employment with the nobility. The middling population, however, would not be denied good food, and so they hired skilled women cooks, known as *cuisinières*, who had mastered the recipes and techniques described in Marin's book and who could produce meals that rivaled those of their snootiest male counterparts.[2]

Marin championed a nouvelle cuisine that was refined, using the freshest ingredients, and his recipes were anything but simple. His sauces, for example, called for precise technique and expensive ingredients. One meat stock required five pounds of veal, a quarter pound of ham, a whole chicken, and beef marrow as well as onions, carrots, and turnips. The result, Marin wrote, should be "soft, unctuous, and of a kind which will be useful to all sauces."[3] Among the many culinary delights Marin popularized are many of the classic French sauces that are still served today, including béchamel, Allemande, Espagnole, supreme, hollandaise, and Soubise, named for the Prince de Soubise, a renowned eighteenth-century gastronome whose meals were so extravagant and delicious that Louis XV was a frequent guest at his dinner table.[4] Marin, in a moment of hyperbole, insisted that a master chef could cook anything and make it delicious. To illustrate his point, he told a story of a caterer whom a group of gentlemen took by surprise when they ordered a dinner at an inopportune moment: the caterer's pantry had no meat or fish of any kind. But he did have an old pair of gloves made from buffalo leather. So he shredded the gloves, stewed them in onions, mustard, and vinegar, and served them to his guests. The gentlemen, having no idea what they had eaten, exclaimed that the meal was a great success.[5]

Not everyone was a fan of Marin's cuisine. The philosopher Jean-Jacques Rousseau was outspoken in his dislike of French food. "The French do not know how to eat," he declared, "because so specialized an art is required to make food eatable to them. . . . Reform the rules of our cooking; have neither flour-thickening nor frying; butter, salt, and diary products should never be put over a fire." He advocated a vegetarian diet of locally grown produce, whatever was in season, prepared as simply as possible. He once said that his ideal meal consisted of "milk, eggs, salad, cheese, brown bread, and ordinary wine."[6] Rousseau's philosophy of the simple life won him a broad audience in the second half of the eighteenth century, but his ideas about diet never gained much of a hold in a nation where gastronomy, the pleasures of savoring lengthy and elaborate meals, was a national pastime. Both upper- and middle-class French men and women adored the gourmet fare that chefs and cooks had raised to an art form throughout the country, and particularly in Paris, which attracted the widest variety of raw products, the most talented chefs, and the most discerning palates from every part of France and beyond.[7]

As the Prince de Soubise knew from personal experience, Louis XV relished the elaborate cuisine of his time. Fortunately for the king, he found a partner who shared his love of all things delicious: Madame de Pompadour, who became Louis's official mistress in 1745. To Madame de Pompadour's many other charms was added her skill as a cook, and she began a new fashion in which royals and nobles prepared meals for intimate dinner parties that welcomed only a handful of guests. At these private suppers, Louis perfected a dish he called *poulet au basilic*, chicken stuffed with chopped basil and other herbs, brushed with raw egg, and then roasted. Leftovers were served to the pages, the young boys who waited on the king and his mistress.

Madame de Pompadour had acquired her taste for fine meals in her bourgeois parents' home. It was said that her ancestors had been grocers and butchers, and the rumors may have been true. Certainly, she knew her way around food and had a discerning palate.[8] Although she encouraged Louis to cook, she also kept a chef de cuisine, whom she challenged to create new dishes. He named one of his culinary inventions after his employer: *filets de volaille à la Pompadour*, or boned chicken breasts that were pounded flat, stuffed with sweet-breads, and braised in bouillon. Because these were royal meals, the chef and his staff used silver cooking utensils and served each course on either silver plates or Sèvres porcelain (a favorite of Madame de Pompadour). This luxury was then imitated by the middle classes as well, and the practice continued to spread. In the late eighteenth century Arthur Young, an Englishman traveling in France, reported that he was surprised to find silverware even in hotel dining rooms.[9]

It was also during this era that "masquerading" became a popular trend in cooking. In an effort to surprise and delight diners, chefs would disguise foods as other foods or sometimes as inedible objects. *Cuisinier Gascon*, a cookbook published in 1740, provided recipes for chicken shaped like bats, veal in the shape of donkey droppings, and something with the unappetizing name of "green monkey sauce." Responding to these types of food in disguise, Voltaire complained: "I detest biting into what appears to be a portion of meat and finding it to be two kinds of rabbit and mostly turkey. . . . And I like a crust on my bread!" Apparently, the rage for refinement had eliminated even that classic of French fare, the crusty baguette. But if the French were losing baguettes, they were gaining pasta, for *Cuisinier Gascon* included recipes for lasagna, ravioli, and gnocchi.[10] For all of Voltaire's grumbling, most French intellectuals enjoyed the elaborate meals characteristic of the age of Louis XV and Madame de Pompadour.

Upon the death of his mistress in 1764, Louis, who by this time had come to equate food with love, took as his new mistress another member of the bourgeoisie, Jeanne du Barry, whose father was a cook.[11] Like her predecessor, Madame du Barry sponsored a new style of cooking, in this case, light, flavorful dishes that appealed to her guests' taste for the novel without leaving them feeling bloated. Another innovation of her kitchen was her choice for chef de cuisine—Madame du Barry hired a woman. Other grand households followed where the king's mistress led, and for the first time in the history of French cuisine, female chefs began taking charge of kitchens in the palaces of the French aristocracy. It was believed they were superior to male chefs because, in part, by the time a male chef was forty years old his palate was no longer reliable, whereas a woman supposedly never lost her ability to detect the subtleties of taste.[12]

Madame du Barry's menus reflected the new simplified style of French cooking. At one dinner prepared for the king, her chef served a pheasant consommé, a ragout of snipe, poached chicken in a cream and butter sauce, roasted chicken with watercress salad, crayfish in Sauternes, and peach ice and strawberries in maraschino washed down by a liqueur made of green walnuts. A persistent legend says that Louis was so pleased with the meal that Madame du Barry asked him to confer upon her chef the *cordon bleu*, an honor formerly reserved for men.[13]

Louis XV's grandson and heir, Louis XVI, did not advance cuisine in France, perhaps because he never had a mistress. Nonetheless, he enjoyed food and ate prodigious quantities at almost every meal. One witness saw him put away in a single sitting an entire chicken, four mutton chops, salad, and six eggs; he finished off the dinner with a single slice of ham.[14] By the 1780s, during Louis XVI's reign, the prime influencers of French cuisine had shifted to the grand ladies who hosted Paris's most glittering salons. Madame Necker, for example, hosted Tuesday night suppers for a select handful of guests who might include the influential Duke of Talleyrand and Madame de Staël. Even in the years and months immediately before the outbreak of revolution, when France was plagued by food shortages, Madame Necker and others of her class continued to enjoy sumptuous meals.[15]

Although he did not like his food disguised or his bread trimmed of its crust, Voltaire did enjoy eating well. It was customary at the time for friends to send one another gifts of food, and from Voltaire's correspondence we know that a dozen baskets of apricots and, on one occasion, an entire wild boar exchanged hands. Writing of a friend who had sent him a gift of game birds, Voltaire said, "His partridges and his ideas have been received—both are good."[16] Voltaire's love for rich food led him to form friendships with fellow gourmands such as the Duke of Richelieu and renowned chefs like Gaspard Grimod de La Reynière, whose grandson would later write a celebrated cookbook, *Almanach des gourmands*. On one occasion Voltaire sent his own chef to study for a while under Grimod de La Reynière. "It is not that I aspire to serve as good fare as you," Voltaire wrote to the chef, "but a cook gets rusty working for a sick man . . . and one must protect the fine arts." Indeed, it appears that the philosopher overindulged in rich food. He complained to a friend, "How good fat hazel-hens are, but how hard they are to digest." Unwilling to give up indulgent meals, he turned to medicine to soothe his indigestion but found that the cure often made him ill. "My cook and my apothecary are killing me," he said.[17] When he invited people to visit, Voltaire promised them especially tasty dishes. "Come and eat our trout and cream," he wrote to one prospective guest while tempting another with "a truffled turkey as tender as a squab and as fat as the bishop of Geneva."[18]

Voltaire's love of food led him to become an avid gardener, and he grew vegetables, fruits, and herbs that in time made their way to his table. Like Jefferson, he sought out seeds for the best varieties—even the German emperor, Frederick the Great, sent seeds to him—and he kept chickens, turkeys, and pheasants (his attempt to raise partridges failed). He promised one visitor "milk from our cows, honey from our bees, and strawberries from our gardens." And, again like Jefferson, he loved wine, especially Beaujolais, on one occasion ordering three thousand bottles.[19]

The late eighteenth century also saw the emergence of an

important new institution—the restaurant. Originally, a restaurant in France was, according to Thomas Corneille's *Dictionnaire universel, géographique et historique* (1708), "a remedy that has the property of restoring lost strength to a sickly or tired individual." Consommés and bouillon were considered excellent restoratives, as were wine, brandy, and cordials. But meat, cooked down to an intensely flavored liquid, was regarded as the best remedy of all. The process called for a large slab of beef, veal, or pork to be put in a large pot and covered with water. The pot was sealed with a tight-fitting lid and set over a low fire to simmer for many hours, until the meat had broken down and formed a rich liquid. Since physicians believed solid food was too difficult for invalids to digest, this liquid meat-essence was an ideal substitute, nourishing and easy on the stomach.[20]

In 1766 the meaning of the word *restaurant* changed from a restorative beverage to a place that sold these types of drinks. The first such establishment was opened in Paris on rue des Poulies by two gentlemen named Roze and Pontaille. The location failed to draw enough business, however, so the partners moved to the bustling rue Saint-Honoré, where they enjoyed tremendous success. Initially, they sold only consommés and bouillons. Their customers sat at small tables, as they would at a wine shop or café, and sipped their restoratives. The business thrived, and Roze and Pontaille soon decided to expand their menu to include light fare such as soups, compotes, pasta dishes, rice, and eggs, all of which were promoted as restoring the health and strength of the weary. They adopted a Latin motto to playfully advertise their restaurant's special offerings: "*Hic saide titillant juscula blanda palatum, / Hic datur effaetis pectoribusque salus*" (Here are tasty sauces to titillate your bland palate, / Here the effete find healthy chests). A weak chest was a common complaint in eighteenth-century Paris and could be symptomatic of anything from asthma and pneumonia to pollen allergies and tuberculosis. Physicians believed that solid food made the blood sluggish, which compounded chest ailments; to keep the blood flowing, they insisted on a liquid diet. The consommés and bouillons served by Roze and Pontaille were just what the doctor ordered.[21]

Before Roze and Pontaille's establishment, there were no restaurants as we know them today, only inns, taverns, or a cook-caterer's shop where the offerings were limited, the cooking indifferent, and the service restricted to specific hours of the day. Joachim Nemeitz, a German gourmand who traveled to Paris in the early 1700s, was unimpressed by the cuisine available in these places. Even more appalling was the public table, a group meal where everyone sat together with no regard for a traveler's desire for privacy, much less respect for the traveler's social rank. Nemeitz soon discovered that people of quality did not frequent public inns; instead, they went to private ones, where they were treated with courtesy and served delicious meals prepared by master chefs.[22]

Nemeitz was not the only critic of the food and service at French inns. In 1763 an ailing Tobias Smollett, the English novelist, passed through France en route to a spa in Italy. He found the food in public inns so abominable that he feared it would kill him before he reached his destination. And in 1790 an Englishwoman, Helen Maria Williams, reported that in spite of the sweeping reforms of the French Revolution, meals at public inns were still awful—so bad, in fact, that she said enduring such miserable fare day after day could drive a traveler to thoughts of suicide.[23]

But travelers were an afterthought in the minds of Parisian innkeepers. Their primary customers were local city dwellers whose apartments lacked a kitchen. These clients went to the inns every day, purchased whatever the kitchen staff had prepared, and carried it home. But if a kitchenless Parisian tired of inn fare, alternatives abounded. The capital was filled with retail food shops where professionals offered a dizzying array of ready-to-eat dishes. *Charcutiers* sold pork, especially sausages. *Rôtisseurs* sold roasted game. *Traîteurs* prepared entire meals and delivered them (it was this arrangement that Jefferson made with Combeaux when he first arrived in Paris). In addition, there were *boulangeries* for bread, *patisseries* for desserts, strolling gingerbread sellers who purveyed their goods in open-air markets, and, of course, wine merchants. You might spend a good deal of time going from shop to shop, but in the end you would have assembled a very good meal.[24]

Within seven years of opening their restaurant, Roze and Pontaille had many imitators, not to mention competitors. In fact, by 1773 Paris had so many restaurants that city officials stepped in to establish standards: the restaurant must be clean; it must serve anyone at any hour of the day; the prices must be fixed and clearly displayed; and it must admit men and women. In the 1770s, Jean-François Vacossin opened a restaurant that became a destination for Parisians as well as travelers from abroad. In the main dining room, he covered the walls with mirrors in conscious imitation of the furnishings at Versailles. His small, private rooms were hung with fashionable landscape paintings that depicted completely imaginary, totally unrealistic scenes of country life, populated especially with young, attractive shepherds and shepherdesses. Vacossin promised his diners healthy food from the purest sources. His water, for example, came from the king's own fountain. His ladyfinger cookies were prepared in the kitchens of the Duke d'Orléans's Palais-Royal. The sugar used in his pastries and custards was imported directly from the plantations of the French colonies in the Caribbean. All dairy products were fresh, and the meat was served not in crude hunks and slabs, but in dainty portions designed to appeal to the delicate appetites and digestion of Vacossin's sensitive clientele.[25]

By the early 1780s, however, fashions had changed. Parisian diners expected hearty meals, and Vacossin tried to keep up with the times, altering his menu to offer chicken fricassee, mutton cutlets, fish stew, and whole roasted chicken. But by this time, bigger restaurants were springing up all around the city. One of the largest, the Cirque du Palais-Royal, located (as its name suggests) in the Palais-Royal, had seating for five hundred, although clients were divided among many private dining rooms designed to accommodate parties of two, four, six, or eight persons.[26]

Menus, too, were becoming increasingly diverse. One of the most popular items being served was the white potato, a relative newcomer to France. In the sixteenth century, the Spanish had encountered potatoes in South America, where the Inca called them *papas*. Tasty, nutritious, easy to store, and simple to cook, this humble root vegetable became a mainstay on Spanish ships. Among its other advantages, the potato also prevented scurvy, a disease caused by a lack of vitamin C, which was rampant among seafarers. Throughout the sixteenth and seventeenth centuries, the potato was introduced to nations across Europe, without much success. Rumors circulated among peasants that it was poisonous and caused tuberculosis, scrofula, syphilis, and even leprosy.

But, ultimately, Europe needed the potato. Unpredictable crop failures and devastating wars that tore the continent apart often caused the starvation of tens of thousands. In the aftermath of the Thirty Years War (1618–48), Europeans looked for crops that would feed the peasants no matter how poor the grain harvest might be. They discovered that the potato was the answer. By the 1740s, monarchs and generals had come to recognize that the potato was also a reliable source of nutrition for their armies. Frederick the Great of Prussia was such an ardent advocate that he had potato seeds distributed free to peasants throughout his kingdom.[27] Within a decade the potato had become standard fare in Prussia, but it was still regarded with suspicion in France. Antoine-Augustin Parmentier, a botanist, was determined to change his compatriots' opinion. During the Seven Years War (1756–63) he had been taken prisoner by the Prussians and survived on a diet made up entirely of the starchy, nutritious potato.

His moment came in 1770, when once again the wheat crop failed in France. The Academy of Besançon offered a prize to anyone who could suggest a new food "capable of reducing the calamities of famine." Parmentier entered the potato in the competition—and won.[28] But he still had a difficult time persuading cooks and consumers that the tuber was safe to eat. Then he hit on an idea that was as sly as it was ingenious. He appealed to Louis XVI for some waste ground where he could plant France's first potato crop. In 1785 the king gave Parmentier forty barren acres at Les Sablons, outside Paris, which he planted with potatoes, ordering the perimeter guarded by troops from dawn until sundown. As Parmentier had hoped, the sight of soldiers standing guard over a field sparked the curiosity of the local people. After dark, some of them crept into the field and dug up some of the potatoes, which they carried home and cooked. The larcenous peasants liked what they had stolen, and so they continued to pilfer the *pommes de terre* and eventually began growing their own.[29]

The potato craze took off. According to legend, the king began wearing the plant's blossoms pinned to his coat, and Marie Antoinette wore a garland of them in her hair. The potato was served at the royal court, which led the aristocracy to adopt it as well. Makers of fine china capitalized on the fashion by painting potato blossoms on dinnerware, and Parisian florists specialized in potato flower arrangements.

Parmentier threw dinner parties at which potatoes were served at every course. Benjamin Franklin was the guest at one such dinner, and scholars believe that Jefferson attended one, too. Street vendors began to sell cooked potatoes to passersby, and soup kitchen fed bowls of healthy potato soup to the poor. Thrilled with the new source of nutritious food, the king told Parmentier: "France will thank you someday for having found bread for the poor." In 1802 Napoleon awarded Parmentier the Legion of Honor; after his death, in 1813, it was customary for many years to plant potatoes on his grave.[30]

Potatoes were not a new ingredient to James Hemings; by this time, the vegetable was already being consumed throughout the United States. But Hemings had other novelties to get used to. For one thing, French kitchens differed significantly from those James had known in America. Back in Virginia, most cooking was done in an open hearth. This method of working over an unprotected fire was risky business, especially because most cooks were women and wore floor-length skirts. Sparks that suddenly exploded from a burning log, or a bit of flaming firewood that rolled out of the hearth, could set a cook's clothes alight. Then there was the sputtering fat from roasts on a spit or from meat in a frying pan, not to mention pots of boiling soups and stews that were prone to tip over. In addition to the dangers presented by the process of cooking, there was the risk inherent in raking, shoveling, and carrying hot coals, among many other possible kitchen mishaps. In 1722 Joshua Hempsted of New London, Connecticut, recorded in his diary that his servant Molly was badly scalded "in ye back & neck" after his son Nathaniel accidentally "spilld a dish of hot milk . . . on her."[31] In France, such accidents were much reduced because most cooking was done over a coal-fired stove.

Other differences distinguished the two countries' food-preparation practices. James had to become accustomed to the large number of men in the kitchen. In Virginia, meals were prepared primarily by women, many of them slaves. It was common for the mistress of a plantation to read a recipe aloud to her cooks and supervise them as they prepared the meals—we know that Martha Jefferson did this. If the meal did not turn out as intended, a master might whip the cook. As a 1712 entry in the diary of the plantation owner William Byrd II of Westover, Virginia, reveals: "I made an indifferent dinner this day because Moll [his enslaved cook] had not boiled the bacon half enough, for which I gave her some stripes."[32]

Thomas Jefferson's Crème Brûlée

We cannot know for certain, but it seems likely that, back at Monticello, James had shown some aptitude for cooking. Why else would Jefferson have taken him to Paris to study French cuisine? Once James became a master chef, Jefferson would run little risk of enduring "an indifferent dinner." As for James, he received an education that was unavailable anywhere in the United States. In terms of variety and quality of meat, produce, wine, and other ingredients, Paris was unrivalled. The city's chefs were the finest in France, which meant that they were among the finest in Europe. Furthermore, there was a culture, an ethos, a philosophy of food in France that did not exist in America. Subtlety of flavor, precise technique, and beautiful presentation mattered to French chefs and diners alike, and James Hemings would master them all.

Chapter 4

THE WINE COLLECTOR
AND RICE SMUGGLER

arly in the morning of a rainy day in February 1787, the Hôtel de Langeac's coachman drove Jefferson's carriage from the stables to the main residence, drawing up the three horses in front of the front door. A few minutes later, Jefferson stepped out of the house accompanied by two servants, one of whom carried his small trunk. The other servant was Adrien Petit, the maître d'hôtel, who would act as Jefferson's personal servant as well as his front man during their upcoming journey, arranging for rooms and meals with innkeepers along the way. Jefferson's "chariot," as he always called it, was enclosed to protect its passenger from not only the weather but also the dust and mire of the roads kicked up by the vehicle's wheels. It was a small carriage and could accommodate only one passenger; Petit probably sat up front with the driver. According to Jefferson's itinerary, they would first head south to Marseille and then eastward over the Alps into northern Italy. All told, Jefferson would cover some twenty-four hundred miles, round-trip, and would not return to Paris until early summer.[1]

In a letter to his protégé and private secretary William Short, Jefferson revealed what he intended to investigate on his grand tour: "Architecture, painting, sculpture, antiquities, agriculture, the condition of the laboring poor."[2] In other words, everything. Yet he also had a more personal reason for traveling to the South of France; five months earlier, he had broken his right wrist while he and his horse tried to jump a fence at the park of Cours-la-Reine in Paris. The physicians bungled the setting of the bones, and, although technically healed, his wrist was still troubling him. Jefferson hoped to find a cure in the spas of the country's warmer climes. Writing to James Monroe he said that he intended "to try the mineral waters there for the restoration of my hand."[3]

As a member of the diplomatic corps and a man of rank, Jefferson would have been justified in taking along a large retinue of servants. On this journey, however, he was not traveling as an American ambassador but as a private citizen, and his entourage was much reduced. As he wrote to his friend John Banister, "I was alone thro the whole, and think one travels more usefully when they travel alone, because they reflect more."[4] Jefferson may have been a tourist, but he was an unusually thoughtful one.

He left the city via the Porte d'Orléans, on the southern perimeter of Paris, and then his coachman turned east toward Dijon. Fifty-five miles from Paris, at Fontainebleau, the wheels gave out, and the group was compelled to spend two days in the town, waiting for the carriage to be repaired. This problem would be a recurrent one throughout the trip, caused mainly by the humpbacked roads of France. The convex bump that stretched along every highway was excellent for draining water from the road, but it threw off the carriage's balance, forcing Jefferson and his servants time and again to interrupt their journey and seek out repairs.

Still, aside from the road surfaces that were hard on Jefferson's carriage, travel through France in the late 1780s was relatively safe and easy. The government had set up post houses every ten miles along all the roads. At these rest points, travelers could hire fresh horses, drivers, guides, and servants; the inn-like establishments also offered meals and lodging for the night. Adding to the overall sense of safety were the mounted troops who patrolled roadways, ensuring that highwaymen did not molest travelers.[5]

Compared to the way most people traveled at the time, Jefferson's style was luxurious. A less-prosperous member of the population would usually buy a seat on a diligence, a stagecoach that typically crammed eight passengers into a tiny compartment. Such journeys were almost always uncomfortable and could be awkward, especially if fellow passengers were in any way unpleasant. Furthermore, riders were at the mercy of the diligence company's schedule, which meant that sometimes they had only a few minutes to gulp down a bit of food and use the post-house privy. Rolling along in his own carriage, attended by servants and able to stop whenever and wherever he liked for as long as he liked, Jefferson was truly among the traveling elite.[6]

On March 3, he and his party reached the historic province of Champagne. The farmer and gardener in Jefferson immediately noticed the soil, which he described as "generally a rich mulatto loam." For seven hundred years, that "mulatto loam" had produced some of the world's finest wines. Back in the eleventh century, Pope Urban II had asserted that the wine of Champagne was the best in the world. As a native of the region, Urban could hardly claim to have an impartial opinion, but over the centuries many wine lovers have agreed with him. In the sixteenth century, Pope Leo X, Charles V of Spain, and Henry VIII of England all purchased vineyards in the region and filled their cellars with its delectable wines.

Of course, these early wines were nothing like the Champagne we enjoy today. The beverage's characteristic bubbles, produced by carbon dioxide released during the fermentation process, were considered undesirable until the early eighteenth century, when Philippe, the duke of Orléans, started a fashion for sparkling wine. The nobility of France followed

Map of France, ca. 1780. The Jefferson party's journey took them southeast through the wine-producing regions of Champagne, Burgundy, Rhône-Alpes, Languedoc-Roussillon, and Provence before detouring into northern Italy.

Philippe's lead, and effervescent Champagne became a popular beverage, especially on festive occasions.[7] By the time Jefferson toured the region, the famous houses of Moët et Chandon, Taittinger, and Veuve Clicquot were already flourishing.

Naturally, Jefferson sampled the renowned wines of Champagne but initially found them not to his taste, leaving this terse assessment in his travel notebook: "wine not good."[8] Given that sparkling wines were then unknown in the United States, his initial prejudice against the bubbles may be forgiven. His aversion did not last long, however. If sparkling wine is an acquired taste, he acquired it pretty quickly, for in April he sampled a Nebbiolo wine, which he praised as being "as brisk as Champagne." As he sampled more and more types, Jefferson came to some astute conclusions about the wine and its production. First, he decided that white pinot grapes made a finer Champagne than did red pinot grapes. Second, contrary to popular opinion at the time, he believed that Champagne was not at its best when consumed young; on the contrary, he felt that cellaring improved its taste. He was fortunate to try some very fine aged Champagnes as revealed in his notes: "1766 was the best year ever known ... 1755 and 1776 next to that. 1783 is the last good year, and that not to be compared with those."[9]

But the trip was not entirely spent imbibing wines. Jefferson had been serious when he told William Short of his intention to study the living conditions of the country's working poor. In a letter to the Marquis de Lafayette, he described his investigation.

"You must ferret the people out of their hovels as I have done," he wrote, "look into their kettles, eat their bread, loll on their beds under pretence of resting yourself, but in fact to find if they are soft."[10] Often what he found did not please him. "I observe the women and children carrying heavy burdens. . . . This is an unequivocal indication of extreme poverty. Men, in a civilized country, never expose their wives and children to labor above their force and sex, as long as their own labor can protect them from it."[11]

After leaving Champagne, the group traveled south to Burgundy, where Jefferson toured some of France's best and most renowned vineyards. He started with Chambertin and then moved on to "Vougeot, Romanee, Vosne, Nuits, Beaune, Pommard, Volnay, Meursault, and end at Montrachet." (These vineyards still produce some of the finest and most sought-after and expensive wines in the world. In 2011, for example, dealers priced a single bottle of 2005 Domaine de la Romanée-Conti at $19,250.[12]) After hiring a pony and a local peasant to serve as his guide, Jefferson explored the region's great wine-producing estates. He had hopes of establishing a vineyard of his own at Monticello, so he expressed interest in every facet of wine-making. Out among the vines he climbed off his pony and dug into the soil to understand the *terroir* of Burgundy. He found that the soil was reddish, mixed with small stones. About a foot below the surface he hit bedrock.

An examination of the soil is important to any wine-maker, but terroir is more than just dirt. To truly study a vineyard's terroir, as Jefferson did, is to examine a complex set of variables and their effects on the vines: the type of soil, its drainage properties, the altitude of the vineyard, the amount of sunlight the vines get each day, and the typical weather conditions of the region. In discussions with vineyard owners and winemakers, Jefferson learned that it took five or six years before a newly planted vine produced enough grapes to make wine. In Jefferson's day, vintners used the same vines for a hundred or, in some cases, one hundred fifty years. By contrast, vines today are torn up when they reach forty or fifty years old.[13]

In Burgundy, Jefferson's favorite wine was Chambertin. He savored its flavor but also its strength. With the stocking of his own wine cellar at Monticello in mind, he wrote in his notebook that it "will bear transportation." Made from the pinot noir grape, Chambertin is one of the *grand cru* wines of France. (*Grand cru* means "great growth" and denotes the highest level of classification of wines from Burgundy.) It is a full-bodied, deeply colored red, with intense flavor of fruit and a rich aroma that some aficionados describe as a medley of cherries, licorice, and musk.

Another great vineyard Jefferson visited was Clos de Vougeot, established by Cistercian monks in the twelfth century. When Jefferson visited the monastery, the monks tended one hundred twenty-four acres of vineyards and produced about fifty thousand bottles a year. Making wine at the monastery was more than a tradition, it was the monks' vocation, and their dedication to it was so complete that by the eighteenth century connoisseurs considered Clos de Vougeot the best wine in Burgundy. Just a few years later, during the French Revolution, the government expelled the monks and sold the vineyard at public auction. Ultimately, eighty individuals owned a parcel of the monks' original vineyard, and all of them tried to make wine. Unfortunately, they lacked the monks' skill, experience, and dedication, and the quality of Clos de Vougeot subsequently plummeted.[14]

Eventually, Jefferson made his way to Beaune, the region's winemaking center, where he made the acquaintance of Étienne Parent, a barrelmaker turned wine merchant. On the subject of fine Burgundies, Parent had no peer. He educated Jefferson on the region's wines and helped the American select the best ones for his cellars in Paris and, later, Monticello. A man like Parent was indispensable in the eighteenth century. At a time before governments had stepped in to establish standards of quality control or connoisseurs had begun publishing guides and dissecting vintages, it was extremely difficult, not to mention confusing, for a nonprofessional to stock a wine cellar. Parent had a discerning palate and years of expertise, which he placed at the service of an eager and appreciative clientele, Thomas Jefferson among them.[15]

From Beaune, Jefferson traveled the short distance to the little town of Meursault, still surrounded by its medieval stone walls.

There he met Jean-Joseph Bachet, who operated a thirteen-acre vineyard named La Goutte d'Or (The Drop of Gold). Bachet's wine became Jefferson's favorite Meursault, and he kept a supply on hand for the last two and a half years he spent in France; indeed, Bachet's Meursault became the house white wine at the Hôtel de Langeac.[16]

Next on the itinerary was the province of Beaujolais. On March 9, amid a fierce rainstorm, Jefferson's carriage drew up before the door of the Château de Laye-Epinaye. Jefferson and the Comtesse de Laye-Epinaye had two friends in common, the Abbé Chalut and the Abbé Arnoux. The clergymen had written a letter of introduction for Jefferson so that he would be received by the countess as a guest (her husband, the count, was in residence at Versailles).[17]

Jefferson stayed at the château for three days, during which time he explored the fifteen-thousand-acre estate. Although the storm prevented him from venturing out on his first day, the two days that followed were clear. Of his experiences, Jefferson wrote: "This is the richest country I ever beheld." Everywhere he rode, he saw well-tended farmhouses covered with slate roofs rather than thatch, and healthy, well-dressed peasants. He examined vineyards, orchards, and wheat fields, all of which pleased him, as well as herds of white cattle, which he thought were "indifferent" compared to the breeds found in America. But, as he had set out to do initially, Jefferson returned to the condition of the peasants, which he found to be entwined with the politics of France. "The people of Burgundy and Beaujolais are well clothed, and have the appearance of being well fed," he wrote. "But they experience all the oppressions which result from the nature of the general government. ...What a cruel reflection that a rich country cannot be a free one."[18]

After full days exploring the estate, Jefferson spent evenings at the château. His hostess was suffering from a heavy cold, but she did her utmost to entertain her guest. Jefferson noted that the countess treated him "with a goodness and ease which was charming." While inside the castle, he came upon a statue of Diana and Endymion by Michelangelo Slodtz, one of the finest French sculptors of the Rococo period. (Another of his works, a statue of St. Bruno, can be found in St. Peter's Basilica in Rome.) Jefferson praised the countess's example of Slodtz's art as "a very superior morsel of sculpture."[19]

Back on the road, Jefferson began following the route that runs along the eastern bank of the Rhône River. The weather was often terrible—the travelers were plagued by heavy rain, freezing temperatures, hail, and even snow. But between Lyon and Nîmes Jefferson found something to distract him from the inclement climate: ancient Roman ruins. At Vienne he visited the former Temple of Augustus and Livia, which had survived virtually intact since the first century, in part because, in the fourth century, it had been converted into a Christian church. Jefferson didn't see it that way. First, he didn't realize the structure had originally served as a pagan temple; he thought it was "the Praetorian Palace." Second, it didn't occur to him that, had the building not been converted to another use, it probably would have been destroyed, either by being mined for its marble or burned to produce lime (such had been the fate of many ancient structures in the Roman Forum). From Jefferson's point of view, this classical monument had been "totally defaced" by the "Barbarians" of the Middle Ages. He lamented the "beautiful, fluted, Corinthian columns cut out in part to make space for Gothic windows." But as he encountered more architectural ruins, his spirits lifted. He later confessed that he was "nourished with the remains of Roman grandeur" and "immersed in antiquities from morning to night."[20]

As the group approached Nîmes, in southern France, Jefferson stopped his carriage and alighted so that he could inspect the spectacular Roman aqueduct known as the Pont du Gard. Once in the town proper, he visited the ruined Temple of Diana and the Roman amphitheater. But by far the chief local attraction for antiquarians was the Maison Carrée, one of the best-preserved Roman temples in Europe. Construction of the building had begun in 16 B.C., and, in about A.D. 2, the temple was dedicated to Caesar Augustus's two adopted sons, Gaius and Lucius. The structure enchanted Jefferson. In a letter to his friend Madame de Tesse, he wrote: "Here I am, madam, gazing whole hours at the Maison quarrée, like a lover at his mistress."[21] Years later, when he was back in Virginia and designing the new state capitol, he would use the long, rectangular shape and classical facade of the Maison Carrée as his model.

But Roman ruins were not the only things admired by Jefferson as he traveled south. Nature, too, inspired him. In spite of the bad weather, the almond trees were beginning to blossom, a spectacular sight. Outside the town of Orange, on the way to Nîmes, he exclaimed, "Here begins the country of olives!" He also noted details of the flora and fauna he came across: "Thyme growing wild here on the hills. Asses very small."[22]

The lure of the vine was never far, however, especially in this viticultural region. As he traveled through the Côtes du Rhône, Jefferson grew fond of the Côte Rôtie wines, made from syrah grapes. He made a note to order bottles for his house in Paris, a significant detail because selling wine by the bottle was a relatively new innovation, only forty or fifty years old. The first wine bottles were not bottles at all but decanters, which were carried down to the cellar and filled straight from the barrel. At the time of Jefferson's journey, wines by the cask were still available, and many consumers preferred to have it delivered that way. Glass containers were liable to break, and the cost of bottling and shipping increased the price by two-thirds. In addition, the bottles were sealed with a piece of cork, and to remove it required a new tool: the corkscrew. Jefferson carried one with him, in the same little case that held his toothbrush.[23]

At the village of Tain-l'Hermitage, north of Nîmes, Jefferson stopped to sample the local wines. According to legend, in 1225 a crusader named Gaspard de Sterimberg returned from the Holy Land with some cuttings of syrah grapevines. After years of warfare, he longed for the quiet life of a hermit, and so he built his hermitage above the village and settled into days divided between saying his prayers and cultivating his vines. Other hermits joined him, forming a loose community of solitaries. The community drew recruits for more than five hundred years, until the last hermit died in 1751. The Hermitage wines delighted Jefferson, particularly the white ones, which tasted a bit like flint with a touch of sugar. He never forgot them. Decades later, when he became president of the United States, Jefferson ordered five hundred bottles of Hermitage white for the White House wine cellar.

Upon leaving Tain-l'Hermitage, Jefferson continued south, passing through a series of poor villages where the laborers lived in huts made of mud and stone. He was shocked to learn that the people rarely ate meat. The villagers had "plenty of cheese, eggs, potatoes and other vegetables and walnut oil for their salad," but most families survived the year on the meat of a single salted hog. Still enforced was the medieval decree that restricted all wild game to the local nobility. A peasant who was caught netting a pheasant, trapping a rabbit, or shooting a deer would be imprisoned for his first offense and executed if he repeated his crime.[24]

In Aix-en-Provence, in France's southernmost Provençal region, Jefferson was able to fulfill one of the goals of his journey—applying the healing mineral water to his sore wrist. Faith in the restorative properties of the mineral springs of Aix dated back at least to the time of the Romans in the first century B.C. The bathhouse Jefferson visited had been built early in the eighteenth century and paved with marble. Throughout the building were brass faucets where visitors could fill their glasses to drink the water or bathe their sores or injuries. For more serious afflictions, private bathing rooms were provided. The English novelist Tobias Smollett, who visited the baths in Aix a few years before Jefferson, reported that the water cured "the gout, the gravel, scurvy, dropsy, palsy, indigestion, asthma, and consumption."[25]

Jefferson bathed his wrist forty times, but "without any sensible benefit," as he wrote to William Short. Healing required patience, as he remarked to his protégé back in America: "My wrist strengthens slowly. It is to time I look as the surest remedy, and that I believe will restore it at length."[26] Any disappointment he felt at not being healed quickly was overshadowed by the pleasure he took in the city and surrounding countryside. "I am now in the land of corn, wine, oil, and sunshine. What more can a man ask of heaven?" As for the town itself, Jefferson was overwhelmingly impressed. "This city is one of the cleanest and neatest I have ever seen in any country. The streets are straight, from 20 to 100 feet wide, and as clean as a parlor floor

. . . [with] rows of elms from 100 to 150 years old, which make delicious walks."[27] The avenue to which all of Aix resorted—natives and visitors alike—was the Cours Mirabeau, considered the most beautiful thoroughfare in Europe. Along the street stood handsome seventeenth- and eighteenth-century mansions; overhead the century-old elms cast their shade over the pavement. It was an elegant setting for that aristocratic custom known as "taking the air."[28] Even in this fashionable town, Jefferson kept to his rule for this journey, declining dinner invitations and avoiding any social interaction with the upper crust. Observing and learning from the peasants and working classes was his primary task: "[I] courted the society of gardeners, vignerons, coopers, farmers, etc and have devoted every moment of every day almost, to the business of inquiry."[29]

On March 20 Jefferson left Aix for Marseille, France's greatest southern port, only twenty miles away. Marseille stood on a grand plain, with mountains at its back and the sea at its feet. Jefferson was charmed by "all the life and activity," which reminded him of London and, perhaps a bit chauvinistically, Philadelphia. He climbed to the hilltop church and monastery of Notre-Dame de la Garde, more to enjoy the view than to visit the sanctuary. One day he took a boat to the island fortress of the Château d'If, which would feature so prominently in Alexander Dumas's 1844 novel *The Count of Monte Cristo.*

Jefferson's friend the Marquis de Chastellux had given him a letter of introduction to Henri Bergasse, one of the foremost wine merchants in France. Bergasse increased Jefferson's knowledge of wine, gave him a tour of his vast wine cellar, and showed him the best way to store wine in bottles: laid on their sides and covered with sand. One night the nobleman threw a dinner party, and Jefferson broke his own rule to attend, spending a happy evening enjoying hearty food, aristocratic company, and a selection of excellent wines.

As was usual throughout his trip, Jefferson continued to scour the local countryside for any produce that might thrive in America. In Marseille he found varieties of figs, seedless grapes that could be dried into raisins, capers, pistachios, and almonds, all of which he believed "may succeed on, or southward of the Chesapeake."[30] Among other things, Marseille did a thriving business exporting Italian rice. Jefferson was impressed that rice from Italy came to market with its kernels clean and whole, unlike the rice grown in America, which often had its kernels broken in the cleaning process. Due to the unattractive appearance of America's "broken rice," European merchants refused to purchase it, knowing that their consumers would not buy it. Jefferson wondered if Italian rice growers had a more efficient cleaning machine unknown in the United States. To satisfy his curiosity, and hopefully to find another European product that would improve life in America and open European markets to American planters, Jefferson made a detour into northern Italy.

Setting out for the border, Jefferson's party first reached

Nice, where they learned that the roads through the Alps were still covered with snow, making a carriage journey impossible. So Jefferson left the vehicle at a stable and hired mules, muleteers, and a guide to lead him and Adrien Petit through the Tende Pass and down into the Po Valley. They set out on April 13, 1787, Jefferson's forty-fourth birthday.

He had chronicled the appearance of crops as he entered Provence; now he reported their absence as he climbed into the Alps. "There are no Orange trees after we leave the environs of Nice. We lose the Olive after rising a little above the village of Scarena on Mount Braus, and find it again on the other side a little before we get down to Sospello. But wherever there is soil enough, it is terrassed and in corn. The waste parts are either in two leaved pine and thyme, or of absolutely naked rock."[31]

The road through the Alps took them to a height of 6,145 feet—the highest point Jefferson had ever been in his life. The sure-footed mules navigated the deep snow easily, and, as in France, post houses appeared every ten or twelve miles, allowing the travelers to rest, warm themselves, and have a meal. When not studying the scenery, Jefferson amused himself by rereading the account of Hannibal's passage through the Alps during his invasion of Italy in 218 B.C. He tried to identify which route Hannibal followed, with his army of seventy thousand men and thirty-seven elephants, but, he lamented, "the descriptions given of his march are not sufficiently particular to enable us at this day even to guess at his tract across the

Alps." After passing through gorges and admiring "a mountain cloven through," Jefferson and his party reached the commune of Limone Piemonte, from which he enjoyed a magnificent view of the Po Valley. Once the group had descended into Italy, Jefferson exchanged his mules and muleteers for a carriage and coachman.[32]

Now began one of the most extraordinary incidents in the life of Thomas Jefferson. While in Lombardy, he visited rice farms and was shown the machine that removed the husks from the grains. It seemed no different from the type of rice-cleaning machines used in America; nonetheless, Jefferson purchased one, intending to send it back to Virginia. What he then discovered was that the rice grown in Lombardy was of better quality than the rough rice grown in America. He wanted to acquire samples to send back to the planters in South Carolina but was told it was impossible—the law forbade the export of seeds from the Lombard rice plants, and the penalty for attempting to transport the grain out of the country was death.

Undeterred, Jefferson took the risk. In a letter to Edward Rutledge of South Carolina he confessed: "I could only bring off as much as my coat and surtout pockets would hold." He knew this amount wasn't enough, so he bribed a muleteer to smuggle sacks of the rice out of Italy. Jefferson's brief career as a rice smuggler never troubled his conscience. Years later, in a memorandum he wrote to himself entitled "Services to My Country," he stated: "The greatest service which can be rendered to any country is, to add an useful plant to its culture."[33]

Returning to Paris, Jefferson followed a different route, through western France. He wanted to see that engineering marvel, the two-hundred-mile-long Canal de Languedoc, which linked the Mediterranean with the Atlantic. (The canal still exists today, although it is known now as the Canal du Midi.) He booked passage on a barge, a voyage that took nine days. He had the wheels removed from his carriage and used it as his stateroom, in which he read, wrote in his notebook, caught up on correspondence, and simply observed the passing scenery. After disembarking, Jefferson had the carriage wheels restored and then rode on to Bordeaux. It was May, and fresh produce was abundant; at his hotel he enjoyed cherries, strawberries, and spring peas. At Amboise, on June 8, the carriage's wheels required repairs yet again, but for the last time. On June 10, 1787, Jefferson was home at the Hôtel de Langeac, after a trip that had lasted three and a half months.

In every way it had been a remarkable and memorable, not to mention productive, journey. By seeing at long last ancient Roman monuments, Jefferson renewed his admiration for the clean classical lines of Greco-Roman architecture. By sampling some of the best vintages of France, he had confirmed his passion for fine wine. And by bringing back a few sacks of bootleg Italian rice, he hoped to boost America's rice trade. He had seen many fruits, grains, nuts, and vegetables that he thought would flourish in the United States, but he was most enthusiastic about the olive. Back at his desk in the Hôtel de Langeac, Jefferson wrote to the South Carolina Society for Promoting Agriculture what Lucia C. Stanton, Monticello's historian, has described as "a three-page paean to the olive, filled with uncharacteristic exclamation points." Gushing with fervor, Jefferson extolled the olive as "the richest gift of heaven . . . one of the most precious productions in nature." Among other benefits, it would get people to eat their vegetables, because the tasty oil was "a proper and codortable nourishment" for greens. Given so many benefits, he believed that the importation and cultivation of olive trees "should be the object of the Carolina patriot."

The gentlemen of the South Carolina Society for Promoting Agriculture were won over, and the first olive tree seedlings arrived in the state in 1791. Unfortunately, they did not flourish in South Carolina's sultry climate, which resembled not in the least the climate of either Provence or Italy. By 1804 the South Carolina olive tree experiment was abandoned.[34]

The Italian rice project also went bust. South Carolina rice planters were reluctant to tear up and destroy their existing stock for an unknown product. Furthermore, they feared that if they planted the foreign-bred rice in addition to American rice, cross-pollination might create an entirely unpalatable and unmarketable hybrid. The American rice problem was resolved only in 1810, with the development of a new, locally produced variety, Northern Carolina Gold. This crop proved so good that Italy lost its near monopoly of the international rice market, a market that American planters dominated until the outbreak of the American Civil War, in 1861.

In other respects, however, the journey through France and into Italy was a success, and not just for Jefferson. What he saw, what he experienced, what he studied, and certainly what he ate and drank helped him sort out what was best and most useful in Europe. It became his intention to take such goods—whether a mechanical rice-kernel cleaner or olive tree seedlings—back home to America, where he hoped they would flourish. Not all of them would, of course. Nonetheless, when he returned to Virginia, Jefferson would not be just a retired ambassador; he planned to be the apostle of European civilization to his beloved country.

Chapter 5

BROTHER AND SISTER, REUNITED

Now that he was back in Paris, Jefferson prepared for the arrival of his daughter Mary (called "Polly" by the family), whom he had been trying to bring over to France since 1785. Upon leaving Virginia in August 1784, he had placed the then six-year-old Polly and her two-year-old sister Lucy in the care of his sister-in-law Elizabeth Eppes and her husband, Francis, at Eppington, their plantation in Chesterfield County, Virginia. In the interim, many things had changed. In a letter dated September 16, 1784, Eppes wrote with news that Polly, Lucy, and two of the couple's own children were ill. "I wish it was in my power to inform you that your children were well. They as well as our own are laid up with the hooping cough. Your little Lucy our youngest and Bolling are I think very ill. Polly has it badly but she sleeps well and eats hartily, tho she is not fallen off in the least. Doctr. Currie is here attending on your children and ours."[1] In January of the next year, the Marquis de Lafayette returned to France from America with a pair of melancholy letters for Jefferson, one from Francis Eppes, the other from the Eppeses' family physician, Dr. James Currie.

The doctor's letter gave Jefferson more details about the case: "I am sincerely sorry my dear friend now to accquaint you of the demise of poor Miss L. [Lucy] Jefferson, who fell a Martyr to the Complicated evils of teething, Worms and Hooping Cough which last was carried there by the Virus of their friends without their knowing it was in their train. I was calld too late to do any thing but procrastinate the settled fate of the poor Innocent. . . . Mr. Eppes lost his own youngest Child from the same Cause and with difficulty Bollings life was saved. Miss P. [Polly] Jefferson got early over it and is now in good health."[2] Elizabeth Eppes had written, too, to offer some consolation to her brother-in-law's grief: "Its impossible to paint the anguish of my heart on this melancholy occasion. A most unfortunate Hooping cough has deprived you, and us of two sweet Lucys, within a week. Ours was the first that fell a sacrifice. She was thrown into violent convulsions linger'd out a week and then expired. Your dear angel was confined a week to her bed, her sufferings were great though nothing like a fit. She retain'd her senses perfectly, calld me a few moments before she died, and asked distinctly for water."[3] This letter fell victim to the uncertainties of the eighteenth-century trans-Atlantic postal delivery system and did not reach Jefferson until May 1785.

Lucy Jefferson and her first cousin Lucy Eppes were buried in the family cemetery at Eppington. Their graves have never been located, although some believe that Jefferson had his child's remains exhumed and reburied in the family cemetery at Monticello. If such a grave exists, it also has never been found. Nabby Adams recorded the unhappy news in her journal: "Mr. J[efferson] is a man of great sensibility and parental affection. His wife died when this child was born, and he was almost in a confined state of melancholy; confined himself from the world and even from his friends, for a long time; and this news has greatly affected him and his daughter [Polly]."[4]

Bereft once again and fearful he would lose Polly to the next epidemic of childhood illness that swept through Virginia, Jefferson decided that she must join him in France. Understandably, the young girl did not want to leave her relatives and the home she had come to know. Jefferson tried to convince her by promising "as many dolls and playthings as you want for yourself, or to send to your cousins." But Polly wasn't buying it. "I am very sorry you have sent for me," she wrote to her father. "I don't want to go to France. I had rather stay with Aunt Eppes." To yet another letter from Jefferson urging her to come to Paris, Polly replied, "I cannot go to France and hope that you and sister Patsy are well." Faced with her father's persistence, Polly gave him an ultimatum: "I want to see you and sister Patsy but you must come to Uncle Eppes' house."[5]

Jefferson was not about to sail back and forth across the Atlantic to satisfy the demands of a child, even if she was a beloved daughter. Instead, he schemed with his in-laws to get her aboard a ship. They booked her passage, making Polly believe she would be sailing with her cousins. In fact, for several days before the ship sailed, the Eppes children stayed aboard the vessel with Polly, playing with her every day. On the day the ship was to sail, Polly was permitted to play until nightfall. Half-asleep, she returned to her cabin, and when she awoke she found herself at sea, her cousins gone and her only escort a Jefferson family slave, fourteen-year-old Sarah Hemings, known as Sally.

Sally Hemings was not the companion Jefferson had in mind to accompany his daughter. He had instructed the Eppeses to find "a careful negro woman" who had already survived a bout of smallpox and therefore would have been immune to the disease. He suggested Isabel Hern, an enslaved domestic servant at Monticello and the wife of David Hern, one of Jefferson's best artisan-slaves. But in May 1787 Isabel had given birth to a girl and fallen ill after the delivery. She was unable to leave her bed, let alone sail to Europe. The Eppeses then selected Sally as Polly's custodian.[6]

Whatever grief Polly experienced aboard ship soon dissipated, thanks to the attentions of Captain Andrew Ramsey and his crew. They became her new playmates, so much so that when the ship docked in England, Polly refused to disembark. But her friend the captain persuaded her that it was time to go, and he took Polly and Sally to London, where John and Abigail Adams were waiting to care for the child until the arrival of her father.[7] Ramsey and his charges arrived at the Adamses' house at Grosvenor Square on June 26, 1787. Polly, an affectionate child of strong attachments, did not want Ramsey to leave, although soon she felt at ease with the Adamses. Two weeks after her arrival, Abigail Adams wrote to Jefferson: "[Polly] is a child of the quickest sensibility, and the maturest understanding, that I have ever met with for her years. . . . She is the favorite of every creature in the House."[8] Even John Adams was taken with the girl. Writing to Jefferson, he assured him, "In my Life I never saw a more charming child."[9]

With Sally Hemings, the Adamses were less pleased. It was not her appearance that troubled John and Abigail. Isaac Jefferson, a slave at Monticello, would later recall that on the plantation she was known as "Dashing Sally" because of her good looks. He also reported that, in complexion, Sally was "mighty near white," and he described her as "very handsome, [with] long straight hair down her back."[10] But, like Jefferson, the Adamses had expected Polly to arrive with a mature nurse; when she did not, Abigail wrote to her friend in Paris. Sally Hemings, she believed, was "a Girl about 15 or 16 . . . the Sister of the servant you have with you." In fact, Sally was only fourteen years old, which probably would have only increased Abigail's anxiety had she known; as it was, she described Sally to Jefferson as "quite a child." To convince her friend that she was not the only one who considered Sally entirely unsuitable to care for a child not yet nine years old, she added: "Captain Ramsey is of the opinion [Sally] will be of so little Service that he had better carry her back with him. But of this you will be the judge. She appears fond of the child and appears good natured."[11]

Apparently, neither Abigail Adams nor Captain Ramsey was aware that, at Eppington, Sally had been assigned to look after Polly. It was customary in the American South to put enslaved children to work once they reached their tenth birthday. As a member of the privileged Hemings family, Sally would never do fieldwork; she would be employed inside the plantation house. It was a sign of Jefferson's esteem for the Hemingses that young Sally became Polly's caretaker and companion.[12]

In the meantime, Polly and the Adamses expected Jefferson to arrive any day to collect the two girls. Instead, they received a letter from him claiming that paperwork that had piled up during his tour of France and northern Italy compelled him to remain in Paris. He was sending his butler, Adrien Petit, to bring Polly and Sally to him.[13] Petit's arrival in London on July 5, 1787, disappointed the Adamses and threw Polly into a sobbing fit. The next day Abigail wrote to Jefferson that Polly had said "it would be as hard to leave me as it was her Aunt Eppes." Indeed,

Fortunately, an effective inoculation against the disease had existed since the early part of the eighteenth century. An English physician named Edward Jenner had observed that dairy workers who contracted cowpox—a much milder disease—were then immune to smallpox. Jenner drew some fluid from a cowpox pustule and injected it subcutaneously into a healthy individual. The human guinea pig promptly came down with a case of cowpox and ever after was immune to smallpox.

In spite of this success, inoculation was regarded with suspicion in some parts of British colonial America. In 1721 riots broke out in Boston when the Reverend Cotton Mather and Dr. Zabdiel Boylston introduced inoculation; there was widespread fear that the two men were spreading the disease rather than preventing it. One night an unknown assailant even hurled a homemade hand grenade at Mather's house. At age twenty-three, Jefferson had traveled to Philadelphia to be vaccinated. Two years later, in 1768, when Dr. Archibald Campbell, a Norfolk County physician, offered inoculations to Virginians, a mob burned his house to the ground. In spite of such violence, the following year, Jefferson—who was then a member of the Virginia assembly—introduced a bill to lift the colonial government's restrictions on smallpox inoculation.[18]

Once Sally Hemings was settled at the Hôtel de Langeac, she began to learn French; it would have been impossible for her to converse with any of the other servants if she hadn't. At one point James, who was serious about becoming fluent in

French, hired a tutor named Perrault, and Sally may have sat in on the lessons, too.

Like her brother, Sally found herself immersed in a strange and exciting world: grand buildings unlike anything she had known in Virginia; ostentatious wealth that made the richest plantation owner appear shabby; markets filled with exotic goods. And then there were the public celebrations in honor of a string of previously unknown holy days and holidays. Carnival, the weeks leading up to the penitential season of Lent, was celebrated with feasting, drinking, and dancing (not to mention general bawdiness), much of it occurring right in the streets and squares of Paris. During Holy Week, fashionable Paris society formed a glittering promenade down the Champs-Élysées to the Abbey of Longchamp, in the suburbs. During the Middle Ages, the parade had been a religious procession that concluded with prayer in the abbey church. By the 1780s, the event had taken on a decidedly secular tone (much to the annoyance of the archbishop of Paris), with the "procession" now an opportunity to see and be seen, and the goal at the abbey not religious devotion but a concert. The Longchamp parade went right past the front door of the Hôtel de Langeac. We know that one year Jefferson invited friends to watch the promenade from his balcony; no doubt the servants went out to see it as well.[19]

On its surface, the hierarchy of French society must have seemed strong and permanent to these visitors from America, but that monolithic appearance was a facade. In fact, the ancien régime was teetering on the edge of an abyss. In a few short years, the French Revolution would bring down the monarchy, the aristocracy, and the Catholic Church. The radicals would attempt to completely reshape life in France, from replacing Christianity with a newly invented cult that worshipped reason to reorganizing the calendar according to the decimal system: the twelve months of the year (each with a new name that reflected the weather typical of that month) would be made up of three ten-day weeks per month (the days of the week were also renamed). The five days left over at the end of the year were declared national holidays. Neither the calendar nor the cult ever caught on.[20]

The ideas that were at the root of the revolution, however, did find a broad audience. Liberty and modernity were common topics in the salons, in theatrical productions, and in discussions in cafés and arguments in taverns. None of this charged atmosphere would have escaped the servants, and talk of freedom and equality must have been as thrilling for James and Sally Hemings as it was for the most wretched French peasant or slum dweller. Count Mirabeau, who would be influential in the Tennis Court Oath that replaced France's three estates system with a national assembly, tackled the subject directly. "The free blacks are proprietors and taxpayers, yet they have not been allowed to vote. And as for the slaves, either they are men or they are not; if the colonists consider them to be men, let them free them and make them electors and eligible for seats."[21] Unlike the abstractness of the reformed calendar, here was an idea worthy of support—recognizing *gens de couleur*, as they were known in France, as human beings deserving of the same rights as whites, including the right to be elected to government office. That was something James and Sally would never have heard proposed in Virginia.

At the time Sally and Polly arrived in Paris, James was in the final months of his apprenticeship. During the spring and summer of 1787, he was studying under the chef for the Prince of Condé, who taught him in the kitchens of the prince's palace in Paris as well as his country château of Chantilly, situated several hours outside the capital. Everything at Chantilly was magnificent and on a grand scale; the stables—said to be the largest in the world—accommodated 240 horses. Louis-Joseph, Prince de Condé, was a Bourbon, a *prince du sang* (prince of the blood), meaning that he was a member of France's royal family; he lived almost as lavishly as the king and Marie Antoinette. On one occasion he gave a supper party at the château, where he and his eight guests were waited on by twenty-five servants. Indeed, meals at Chantilly had been sumptuous since the seventeenth century, when Louis XIV would come to dine. As a result, Hemings's training in the culinary arts under the prince's chef meant that he was learning the most sophisticated techniques of French cuisine from an absolute master.[22]

Of course, training under the tutelage of a master chef did not come cheap. The prince's chef demanded twelve francs per day, although that sum included James's room and board at Chantilly. Jefferson balked a bit at the hefty fee. His friend Philip Mazzei had made all the arrangements but failed to inquire exactly how much the chef would charge for private cooking lessons. Even if the lessons cost more than Jefferson had expected to spend, he was certainly getting his money's worth.[23]

When he entered Condé's kitchen, James joined a staff made up exclusively of men. What the French upper classes desired—as did Thomas Jefferson, for that matter—was haute cuisine: refined, imaginative dishes served with style. In the homes of the Prince de Condé, stylish service required a host of additional servants. For example, the meat was carved tableside by the *écuyer trenchant*, or carver, who appeared in the dining room in opulent formalwear known at the time as court dress. The carver, along with all the other servants who brought food and drink to the table, was supervised by the maître d'hôtel, or steward, who in the prince's household would have been a nobleman.[24]

James was studying under the prince's chef de cuisine, the head or executive chef, who directed all the activity in the kitchen. Below him was the *officier de bouche*, who supervised the cooks making cold dishes and desserts. Next in line was the maître d'hôtel, who ensured that the kitchen was supplied with everything necessary to prepare superior meals for the prince and his guests. This organizational hierarchy spawned the stereotype of the temperamental chef—the perfectionist who flies into a rage if the least thing goes awry in his kitchen. That label has endured, from Anatole, the overwrought French chef of P. G. Wodehouse's Jeeves and Wooster stories, to that bad boy of reality television, Gordon Ramsey.

In late-eighteenth-century France, a chef de cuisine not only had to be a master of his art—and it was not uncommon for fine chefs to be described as artists—he also had to be a gifted manager, with a genius for consistently getting the best work out of a large and diverse staff. In other words, his administrative skills had to be on a par with his culinary skills.

Elaborate meals prepared entirely by men was a phenomenon unknown in America or England, where people of all classes ate the same thing—meat, some fish, cheese, white bread, a few vegetables, and lots of sweet desserts. Furthermore, these meals were prepared by both male and female cooks working side by side.[25] In colonial America, it was women—not men—who ran the kitchens and wrote the cookbooks, such as *American Cookery* (1796) by Amelia Simmons of Hartford, Connecticut, and, later, Mary Randolph's *Virginia Housewife* (1824).

Assuming that James Hemings had some experience in the Monticello kitchen, he would have been accustomed to cooking with cast iron pots and pans. Brass and copper cookware were available in America, but these articles were pricey. By contrast, in France, copper was the cookware of the professional chef, and it came in every conceivable shape and size, from simple sauté pans to kettles to dessert molds to the long lozenge-shaped pans, known as *turbotieres*, used for cooking fish. Copper conducted heat better than cast iron, and it was more durable. Iron is a fragile metal—dropped on a brick or stone floor, it is likely to crack and thus become useless. The same fall might dent a copper pot, but it wouldn't ruin it.

James was also shown how to operate kitchen equipment that did not exist in America, such as a macaroni maker. In the eighteenth century, macaroni did not refer solely to elbow-shaped noodles; all forms of pasta were called by this term. Legend claims that Marco Polo brought macaroni to Europe from China, but food writer and James Beard Award winner Clifford A. Wright has discovered that Arabs were the first to make pasta and that it came to Europe via Sicily, where in the twelfth century cultural exchanges among Arabs, Greeks, Normans, and Sicilians were thriving. In addition to becoming adept with new tools and machines, James grew familiar with ingredients unavailable in America, including truffles, olive oil, and the sparkling wine known as Champagne.[26]

Several weeks after completing his studies with Condé's chef, Jefferson appointed James chef de cuisine at the Hôtel de Langeac. The kitchen was his domain; he was now a man of authority, with a staff who answered to him. In recognition of James's new position, Jefferson increased his salary. As a trained chef, James knew of still more ways he could supplement his income. France had a burgeoning market for grease, animal fat, and animal skins, and it was one of the perquisites of a chef to sell these kitchen byproducts and pocket the proceeds. And that's exactly what James did.[27]

Jefferson entertained often at the Hôtel de Langeac, and each dinner party was an opportunity for James to display his newly acquired skills. These events could be incredibly stressful. "The French," as the historian Annette Gordon-Reed has observed, "were as serious about their cuisine as about fashionable attire. In fact, the two were closely related, since the presentation of food—the look—took its place alongside taste as a mark of true distinction. Every dish Hemings prepared invited a judgment by a man who was a perfectionist."[28]

One of James's first dinner parties was given by Jefferson in honor of Maria Cosway, an English artist, musician, and socialite for whom Jefferson developed a serious romantic attachment. (Cosway was married, but her husband was unfaithful; historians still argue whether she and Jefferson had an affair.[29]) The two became close friends and often went sightseeing together. In the fall of 1786, when Cosway was obliged to leave Paris for a time, Jefferson suffered a bout of melancholy that made him "the most wretched of all earthly beings." To console himself and amuse Cosway, he wrote "The Dialogue between My Head and My Heart," in which Jefferson's reason debates with his emotions regarding how best to react to the departure of a dear friend.

For his party, Jefferson drew up a glittering guest list that was top-heavy with distinguished Polish aristocrats (Cosway had many Polish friends in Paris). Among the guests were Princess Lubomirski, a member of one of Poland's wealthiest and most aristocratic families; Count Stanislaus Kostka Potocki, a notable art collector; and Julian Niemcewicz, a poet, play-wright, and statesman. Jefferson also invited Baron Pierre-François Hugues d'Hancarville, a successful dealer in art and antiquities, particularly those freshly plucked from the ruins of Pompeii and Herculaneum.

We do not know what James prepared for Jefferson's guests, but we can assume the dinner was a success because he retained his position as chef de cuisine. At another such soirée, Jefferson entertained the Duke de la Rochefoucauld-Liancourt, an aristo-crat who was sympathetic to democracy. The duke left us no ap-praisal of the meal, but he did share something of his impression of his host: "In private life Mr. Jefferson displays a mild, easy and obliging temper, though he is somewhat cold and reserved. His conversation is of the most agreeable kind, and he possesses a stock of information not inferior to that of any other man."[30]

We also know a few of the recipes that James mastered in France—eight of them, written in his own hand, have survived. There were many more, of course, which he prepared for Jef-ferson, and about one hundred fifty of them have come down to us, passed down by Jefferson or his granddaughters. Some of these dishes have become American classics: fried potatoes, better known as French fries; burnt cream, or crème brûlée; and macaroni with cheese. There is no consensus among culinary historians whether James Hemings and Thomas Jefferson were the first to introduce macaroni and cheese to America; perhaps they did not, but Jefferson served it often at Monticello and later at the White House, which went a long way toward establishing its popularity in the United States. The Library of Congress preserves the manuscript of Jefferson's recipe for making fresh macaroni, the basis for any great mac and cheese dish:

> *6 eggs. yolks & whites.*
> *2 wine glasses of milk*
> *2 tb of flour*
> *a little salt*
> *work them together without water, and very well.*
> *roll it then with a roller to a paper thickness*
> *cut it into small pieces which roll again with the*
>   *hand into long slips, & then cut them to a*
>   *proper length.*
> *put them into warm water a quarter of an hour.*
>   *drain them.*
>   *dress them as maccaroni.*
> *but if they are intended for soups they are to be*
>   *put in the soup & not into warm water*[31]

As for French fries, Jefferson knew them as *pommes de terre frites à cru, en petites tranches,* or potatoes deep-fried while

Maccaroni.

The best maccaroni in Italy is made with a particular sort of flour called Semola, in Naples: but in almost every shop a different sort of flour is commonly used; for, provided the flour be of a good quality & not ground extremely fine, it will always do very well. a paste is made with flour, water & less yeast than is used for making bread. this paste is then put, by little at a time, viz. about 5. or 6 ℔ each time into a round iron box **ABC**

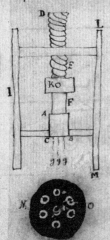

the under part of which is perforated with holes, through which the paste, when pressed by the screw **DEF**, comes out, and forms the Maccaroni ggg. which, when sufficiently long, are cut & spread to dry. the screw is turned by a lever inserted into the hole K, of which there are 4. or 6. it is evident that on turning the screw one way, the cylindrical part **F** which fits the iron box or mortar perfectly well, must press upon the paste and must force it out of the holes. **I.L.M.** is a strong wooden frame, properly fastened to the wall, floor & ciding of the room.

N.O is a figure, on a larger scale, of some of the holes in the iron plate, where all the black is solid, and the rest open. the real plate has a great many holes, and is screwed to the box or mortar: or rather there is a set of plates which may be changed at will, with holes of different shapes & sizes for the different sorts of Maccaroni.

Undated "maccaroni" press design by Thomas Jefferson. The text reads, in part: "The best pasta in Italy is made with a particular sort of flour called [illegible], in Naples: but in almost every shop a different sort of flour is commonly used; for, provided the flour be of a good quality, & not ground extremely fine, it will always do very well." (Courtesy Library of Congress, Manuscript Division, Thomas Jefferson Papers) raw, in small cuttings. Of course, baking macaroni with cheese and frying potatoes were among the humbler dishes Hemings had mastered, and they would be among the easiest recipes he would teach to his apprentice when he and Jefferson returned to Monticello.

Chapter 6

BOILING POINT

T he year Patsy Jefferson turned sixteen, she decided to convert to Catholicism and become a nun. The news caused a sensation among Jefferson's friends and acquaintances, in France as well as in the United States. As the archbishop Antonio Dugnani, papal nuncio to the French court, wrote to Father John Carroll (soon to be the first bishop of Baltimore): "The eldest seems to have tendencies toward the Catholic religion. She is only sixteen. Her father, without absolutely opposing her vocation, has tried to distract her."[1]

Anti-Catholicism was one of the most deeply rooted prejudices in England, and the colonists successfully transplanted it to America. Since the reign of Elizabeth I (1559–1601), English Catholics had been barred from practicing their faith and were heavily fined each time they failed to attend Protestant church services. It was against the law for parents to have their children baptized by a Catholic priest, to teach their children the Catholic faith, or to send their children overseas for a Catholic education. Catholic priests who entered the country, said Mass, heard confessions, performed marriages, gave last rites to the dying, or reconciled Protestants to the Catholic church risked the death penalty. English Catholics who welcomed priests into their homes risked the same punishment. By the 1780s these laws were still on the books in England, but they were rarely enforced. English Catholics lived quietly on the fringe of society. They were barred from attending Oxford or Cambridge universities and could not participate in the political life of their country, but the more punitive Elizabethan penal laws were no longer imposed upon them.

Life for Catholics in America was a different story. When the American Revolution began in 1775, the practice of the Catholic faith was illegal in all thirteen colonies but one— Pennsylvania. Priests from Pennsylvania traveled in disguise and under an alias to minister to scattered congregations in those colonies where priests and Catholicism were outlawed. Even after the ratification of the Bill of Rights, with its guarantee of freedom of religion, some states tried to circumvent the Constitution and bar American Catholics from public office. In New York state, this movement was led by John Jay, future first chief justice of the Supreme Court.[2] Even Jefferson succumbed to the old suspicion that all Catholic priests were hypocritical schemers. In a letter to Horatio Spafford he wrote, "In every country and in every age, the priest has been hostile to liberty. He is always in alliance with the despot, abetting his abuses in return for protection to his own."[3]

On April 18, 1788, Patsy formally requested her father's permission to join the nuns at the Abbaye de Panthemont. Jefferson sent no reply. Instead, he took her shopping and spent more than one thousand francs on new clothes and shoes for her.[4] He also permitted her to attend balls and other entertainments. If his aim had been to make his daughter give up her religious vocation by enticing her with the pleasures of the world, it worked; Patsy abandoned any thought of changing her religion and becoming a nun. Once the problem was resolved, Jefferson visited the Abbaye de Panthemont and, after a brief conversation with the abbess, withdrew Patsy and Polly from the convent school.

Soon afterward, Jefferson found himself facing a complication involving James Hemings. After twenty months of supplemental private French lessons with Monsieur Perrault, James had suspended his studies, which he had paid for out of his own pocket. James still owed Perrault twenty-four livres but refused to pay (no one knows why). On January 6, 1789, Perrault showed up at the Hôtel de Langeac to collect the money owed to him. The meeting between the teacher and his former pupil did not go well. In a letter to Jefferson, Perrault (who refers to himself in the third person), described what ensued: "[James] attacked him [Perrault] with kicks and punches, which forced him to take to his bed since that time, and tore an overcoat from him which is the only article of clothing he has against the rigors of the season, thus putting it out of his power to earn his living, since it is so cold and he daren't appear with his clothes in pieces. Please help him recover his salary, he having always acted well in your respectable house." Then, switching to the first person, Perrault added: "Your porter was a witness, as were others of the ignominious treatment I received at your hotel."[5]

These domestic dramas in the Jefferson household were being played out against the backdrop of a much grander and ultimately tragic crisis. All across France, and especially in Paris, discontent with the government had been simmering for years; in 1789 the pot finally boiled over. The causes of the French Revolution are complicated, but the crippled finances of the government and the outrageously unfair system of taxation played a large part in driving the people to rebellion. Under the rules of the system, the middle and working classes bore the full weight of taxation, while the aristocracy and the Catholic clergy were exempt. Time and again, Louis XVI had brought in a financial advisor to revive France's treasury. All of them told the king the same thing: the system of taxation must be reformed. For stating this inconvenient truth, each advisor was fired. Then, in 1783, the king accepted what he had denied for years—France's tax system was broken. He turned to Charles de Calonne to fix it. Calonne was a lawyer with a strong business sense, and immediately he set about raising revenue—partly by building the wall around Paris and installing customhouses for the collection of duties.

It wasn't enough. France was 113 million livres in debt, and collecting taxes on baskets of eggs and buckets of milk brought into the capital from the countryside wasn't going to fix the problem. In 1787 the king called upon the aristocracy and the clergy to attend an Assembly of Notables, at which Calonne would present his plan to make France solvent again. Among other things, he argued in favor of a universal tax on land. While this proposal seems eminently fair to us today, the assembled notables knew there would be consequences—mainly, that they would no longer be exempt from paying taxes on their vast estates. Calonne's initiative failed.[6]

Desperate for a solution that would save the treasury and perhaps his monarchy, in 1789 Louis XVI called for a meeting of the Estates-General. This body, first created in the fourteenth century, was the closest thing feudal France had to a parliament. It was made up of the three levels, or estates, of society—the clergy, the aristocracy, and the commoners—and it had not been in session since 1614. Rather than tackle the problems afflicting the nation, the three estates spent weeks arguing about their particular powers and privileges.

Not everyone was impressed by Louis's calling of the Estates-General. Chrétien-Guillaume de Lamoignon de Malesherbes, a sixty-eight-year-old statesman who had been working for government reform for decades, dismissed the assembly as "a vestige of ancient barbarism" and called upon Louis to grant France a constitution. "A King who submits to a constitution feels degraded," Malesherbes wrote, "a King who proposes a constitution obtains instead the highest glory among men and their liveliest and most enduring gratitude."[7] Malesherbes was calling upon an absolute monarch to voluntarily become a constitutional monarch, and that Louis would not do.

The debates in the Estates-General especially taxed the patience of the members of the third estate, the commoners. They represented the ordinary populace of France, which vastly outnumbered the nobles and the clergy. Yet in the Estates-General, each estate had a single vote, and the clergy and the nobles always voted together against the commoners. So on June 20, 1789, six hundred delegates of the third estate walked out on the proceedings. At a nearby indoor tennis court—the only building in the neighborhood large enough to hold them all—the delegates declared the Estates-General abolished and the creation of a new sovereign legislative body: the National Assembly. In essence, the commoners had declared that Louis XVI no longer had any authority in France, that the legitimate government was now in the hands of the people.

Would the king give up his power without a fight? Would he send his troops into the streets of Paris to slaughter the delegates of the National Assembly and their supporters? Fear and uncertainty swept through the slums and working-class districts of the capital, and one royal bastion in particular became the object of their paranoia: the Bastille prison.

Built in the fourteenth century as a fortress, by the eighteenth century the Bastille was a prison for the better class of criminals, such as aristocrats, political dissidents, and authors, publishers, and booksellers who disseminated works the government considered indecent or seditious. This huge fortress, with cannons pointed toward the surrounding neighborhoods, became Paris's most important symbol of royal despotism. Rumors spread of dozens of prisoners confined in underground dungeons (in fact, in July 1789, the Bastille held only seven inmates, all of whom were free to walk in the open air atop the building's battlements).

One of the prisoners was the Marquis de Sade, the notorious libertine and author of pornographic novels. During her weekly visits, Sade's wife brought him updates of the political situation. Now when he took the air, he shouted down to passersby brief speeches in favor of the new National Assembly. When the guards retaliated by keeping Sade locked in his cell, he shouted his speeches through the opening in the floor that served as his toilet. Historian Simon Schama tells us that the opening was lined with metal, which made it a natural megaphone. When Sade claimed that Bernard-René de Launay, the governor of the Bastille, was planning to massacre all the prisoners and called upon to people of Paris to save them, de Launay transferred Sade to another prison.[8]

The rumors and unrest in Paris were making de Launay and men like him nervous. The commandant of the Invalides, a hospital and residence for military veterans, sent thirty thousand pounds of gunpowder to the Bastille for safe-keeping. De Launay had only eighty-two men to defend the prison; he begged for reinforcements but received only thirty-two Swiss mercenaries. Although the building was as massive a work of medieval masonry as one could find in Paris, protected by a moat and armed with thirty pieces of artillery, it had no well or spring to provide water and only enough food to feed the garrison and prisoners for two days. De Launay had not been shortsighted; he simply never imagined that one day French citizens would besiege the prison.

On the night of July 13, a rumor circulated that royal troops were on the march against the people of Paris. The next morning a crowd of approximately nine hundred, most of them workingmen from the adjacent Faubourg Saint-Antoine, gathered outside the Bastille. They wanted the gunpowder and they wanted to spike the artillery so the guns could not be used against them by the royal troops, who the rumormongers still insisted were on their way.[9]

De Launay invited two delegates into the Bastille to discuss the crowd's demands. The delegates joined the governor for lunch, but by the end of the meal the two parties had agreed on nothing. On leaving the Bastille, the delegates declared they would go to the Hôtel de Ville, Paris's city hall, for further instructions. Once they were gone, the restless crowd surged into the prison's undefended outer courtyard, crying, "Give us the Bastille!" A few of the more agile protestors climbed up and cut the drawbridge chain, and as the massive bridge slammed down, the crowd ran into the heavily defended inner courtyard, where they were met by gunfire.

The battle raged all afternoon, with the crowd receiving reinforcements from soldiers who had deserted from the royal ranks. They brought along muskets from the Invalides armory, as well as two cannons. By five in the afternoon, de Launay had concluded that further resistance was useless. He raised a white handkerchief over the Bastille, ordered his men to cease firing, and sent out a note demanding safe conduct for himself and his troops and threatening to blow up the gunpowder if it was not given. Such an explosion would have leveled the Bastille and most of the Faubourg Saint-Antoine; nonetheless, the crowd rejected de Launay's terms. Once again, they stormed the fortress, and this time they captured it.[10]

The Bastille garrison had killed eighty-two members of the mob and wounded an unknown number of others. The garrison's casualties were one killed and three wounded. Once the Bastille was in the mob's hands, some members freed the prisoners while others lynched two guards. De Launay was dragged through the streets to the Hôtel de Ville, where the mob shouted suggestions on how best to kill him. When a pastry cook named Desnot spoke in favor of clemency, de Launay cried, "Let me die," and kicked his would-be savior in the groin. At that, the mob attacked the governor, hacking him to death with swords and bayonets looted from the Bastille. Once de Launay was dead, a member of the crowd cut off the corpse's head. It was impaled on a pike, and the mob, singing and dancing around it, carried their gruesome trophy through the streets.[11]

That night, about eleven o'clock, Jefferson's friend the Duke de La Rochefoucauld-Liancourt asked to see the king. After he had described the fall of the Bastille and the murder of Governor de Launay, Louis XVI asked, "It is a revolt?" "No, Sire," the duke replied. "It is a revolution."[12]

The French people as a whole had enchanted Jefferson. In a letter to Elizabeth House Trist, a friend in Philadelphia, he wrote: "The roughness of the human mind are so thoroughly rubbed off with them that it seems as if one might glide thro' a whole life among them without a jostle." It saddened him to see that such a delightful people were ruled by such a corrupt, despotic government. "Of twenty millions of people supposed to be in France," he continued, "I am of the opinion there are nineteen millions more wretched, more accursed in every circumstance of human existence, than the most conspicuously wretched individual in the whole United states." The majority of the French people were the victims, he said, of "a monstrous abuse of power under which these people were ground to powder."[13] Everywhere he looked he saw institutions that kept France poor, ignorant, and backward. He blamed the unjust system of taxation, the government-granted monopolies that crippled industry and any entrepreneurial spirit, the infringement on freedom of religion, speech, and the press, the indolence and decadence of the clergy, and "the enormous expenses of the Queen, the princes & the Court."[14] When Trist showed this letter to James Madison, he suggested that she keep it to herself. Such strong words from a diplomat could cause embarrassment to both Jefferson and the U.S. government.

During the 1780s, Marie Antoinette had become France's national scapegoat. A foreigner, the daughter of the Austrian empress Maria Theresa, the queen was said to have siphoned millions from the French treasury and smuggled the money out of the country to enrich her brother, Emperor Joseph. A stream of salacious pamphlets portrayed the queen as a woman of insatiable sexual appetites who exhausted her male and female lovers, among them the king's brother, the Comte d'Artois. In drunken orgies she took on her entire retinue of bodyguards. A play produced in 1789, *La Destruction de l'Aristocratisme*, had Marie Antoinette's character declare that she hated her French subjects so intensely that "with what delight would I bathe in their blood." Jefferson was no fan of the queen. He believed she was profligate and autocratic—and she was—but it is unlikely that he put much faith in this scurrilous propaganda against her.[15]

Even if he did not think of Marie Antoinette as a sexual omnivore, Jefferson disapproved of her public demeanor. To relieve the boredom of life at Versailles, she surrounded herself with gentlemen known as *chevaliers servants*. Her favorite was the elegant, charming, and enormously wealthy Comte de Vaudreuil. Most of France assumed he was her lover, although Jefferson did not.[16] In a 1787 letter to James Madison he described the queen as "devoted to pleasure and expense," then added that she was "not remarkable for any other vices."[17]

It was her conduct in general that earned Jefferson's disapproval. In dress, the queen preferred the loose, casual, "pastoral" style that was in vogue; Jefferson favored that style for women, just not for a monarch. A queen was not an ordinary individual; she was an embodiment of the nation, and as such her attire should be formal. Then there was the queen's social life: her circle of chevaliers made her a subject of gossip, as did her frequent appearances at the theater; even worse was her appearance on the stage of the theater she had built at her retreat at Versailles, the Petit Trianon. In Jefferson's view, Marie Antionette was still a wife and mother, and her proper sphere was the home, creating a happy family life.

In April 1789, three hundred fifty workers at a Paris wallpaper factory and a nearby saltpeter factory went on strike, protesting their starvation wages of twenty-five sous per day. Some of the strikers cobbled together a gibbet and paraded it through the streets, with effigies of the factory owners dangling from the crossbeam. The protest spread until three thousand men and women were rampaging through the streets.

They attacked the home of the owner of the saltpeter factory, dragged all his fine possessions into the street—including his personal library of fifty thousand books—and burned them. Then they stormed the wallpaper factory and destroyed it. The Gardes Françaises, or National Guard, was called out. In the confrontation between the king's troops and the rioters, twelve soldiers and dozens of rioters were killed.[18]

In this foretaste of the French Revolution, Jefferson's sympathies lay with law and order rather than the aggrieved workers. In a letter to John Jay, he characterized the demonstrators as a "mob . . . the most abandoned banditti" whose actions were "unprovoked and unpitied."[19]

By July, Jefferson's mood had swung from partisan to dispassionate observer. On the afternoon of July 13, the day before the storming of the Bastille, he was riding in his carriage through the Place Louis XV (soon to be the location of the guillotine). At one end of the square were Louis XVI's mercenary German cavalry; at the other end stood a crowd of Parisians armed with stones. The crowd parted so that Jefferson's carriage could pass, then closed ranks again, and a moment later attacked the Germans. As historian William Howard Adams describes it: "In that file of sullen, defiant Frenchmen, Jefferson had made his closest contact with the raw forces of the French Revolution."[20]

After Jefferson's brush with the Paris mob on July 13, events accelerated within the city. The next day, the Bastille was captured and its governor and two of his deputies were murdered. On July 15 the Marquis de Lafayette was named commander of the Gardes Françaises and swore before the high altar in the Cathedral of Notre-Dame to defend the liberty of the people. On July 16, Jefferson watched as Lafayette and his troops escorted Louis XVI and fifty deputies into Paris. It was estimated that sixty thousand Parisians lined the route, and most of them were armed—some with scythes, others with swords or pistols looted from the Bastille or the Invalides. The royal government's progress across the city, through a grim and suspicious multitude, must have been an ordeal for the king, and it ended with a humiliating gesture—he was obliged to pin to his hat a red, white, and blue ribbon, the cockade of the revolution.

Two weeks later, Jefferson concluded that the mob was harmless. "I have been thro' [the city] daily," he wrote to a friend, Count Diodati, "have observed the mobs with my own eyes in order to be satisfied of their objects, and declare to you that I saw so plainly the legitimacy of them, that I have slept in my house as quietly thro' the whole as ever I did in the most peaceful moments."[21] He was confident that from then on the work of drafting a constitution and forming a republic would distract the Parisians "from the bloody objects which have lately occupied their minds."[22]

In August, Lafayette begged Jefferson to host a dinner party for various delegates who represented the increasingly fragmented political factions in the National Assembly. Some delegates wanted the king to possess the power of veto; at the other end of the spectrum were those who wanted the king to have no political power at all. Between the two extremes were a host of other points of view. Lafayette hoped that civil war could be averted by rational discussion over a good dinner served at the home of a man whose Declaration of Independence had inspired lovers of liberty in every nation of Europe. The dinner party lasted six hours. Afterward, Jefferson concluded that James Hemings's food and his own wines had done the trick. He noted that the discussion among the delegates had been marked by "logical reasoning and chaste eloquence." The gentlemen were willing to compromise, and soon, he predicted, France would have "a good constitution."[23]

Also that month, Jefferson received a letter from James Madison in which his friend wrote: "I have been asked if any appointment at home would be agreeable to you."[24] The implication was unmistakable—he was being offered a position in the first-ever administration of President George Washington. Jefferson replied, "[When] I quit the present, it will not be to engage in any other office."[25] As Jefferson prepared for his departure from France, he suddenly came down with a violent migraine headache that kept him confined to his bed for six days. Studying other occasions when Jefferson was incapacitated by a migraine, the biographer Fawn Brodie believes there is a pattern to these afflictions: "It was triggered, it would seem, by a sense of loss." In the five years Jefferson lived in France, he never had a single migraine, but now that he was going home, "he was losing friends, artists, scholars, scientists, Paris—all of Europe—to say nothing of a place in the new French Revolution."[26] For his illness in Paris, Jefferson was attended by a seventy-two-year-old Welsh doctor named Richard Gem, whom Jefferson considered one of the most skillful physicians he had ever met. But perhaps his recovery had less to do with Dr. Gem's prescriptions and more to do with Jefferson's own acceptance of the inevitable: he was leaving France.

The last dinner party at the Hôtel de Langeac took place the evening of September 17, 1789. Jefferson had invited four guests: the Marquis de Lafayette, the Duke de La Rochefoucauld, the Marquis de Condorcet, and an American, Gouverneur Morris. All four men believed in democratic government and welcomed the first signs of revolution in France.

Condorcet was an eccentric polymath who was perennially nervous and volatile, even among his friends. In a city obsessed with style, he dressed in shabby clothes and wore his hair cropped unfashionably short. But Jefferson liked him, perhaps because, in the 1770s, Condorcet had been one of the first men in France to express his support for America's revolution.[27]

Morris was a New York aristocrat, an ardent American patriot, and the author of much of the language in the United States Constitution. He had come to Europe to increase his international business contacts. Morris was also a playboy; at the time of Jefferson's farewell party, he was sharing a mistress, the Comtesse de Flahaut, with that political and religious chameleon Charles de Talleyrand, who at this stage of his career was bishop of Autun. In his diary, Morris recorded an evening the three lovers spent together: "[The comtesse's] Countenance glows with Satisfaction in looking at the Bishop and myself as we sit together agreeing in Sentiment & supporting the Opinions of each other. What Triumph for a Woman! I leave her to go Home with him and thus risque heroically the Chance of Cuckoldom. What Self Denial for a Lover."[28]

La Rochefoucauld was a scholar who dabbled in chemistry, a political liberal, and, in spite of his exalted rank, an affable self-effacing man. In addition to sharing the same political views, he and Jefferson were both interested in using scientific methods to make their farms more productive.[29]

Lafayette was the last guest to arrive. He and Jefferson had met in America, where the latter had been put off by the vanity of the young marquis. He once characterized Lafayette's craving for fame and attention as a "canine appetite." In Paris, however, Lafayette had won over Jefferson by his many acts of kindness, so much so that the two men developed a lasting friendship.[30]

The dinner conversation revolved around the disturbing news of the day. The shortage of bread in Paris had become so critical that soldiers were posted outside bakers' shops. A rumor was spreading across the city that the king was preparing to flee to the garrison town of Metz and raise an army to seize the government. There was unrest among the troops, and no one could say with certainty if the soldiers were loyal to Louis or to the new National Assembly. Lafayette, who had command of some of the troops in Paris, assured his friends that his men would march out and fight for the new government—provided that it wasn't raining.[31]

We do not know what James Hemings prepared that day (the meal began at four in the afternoon), but we do know how the food was served. Jefferson had adopted a new French fashion: between each seated guest was a small table. As each course was served, servants placed the platters and bowls on the tables; then the servants left the dining room, and each guest helped himself. The purpose of this custom was to encourage free and open conversation, which might not occur if servants were present.[32]

Jefferson was planning to leave Paris on September 26, but he did not tell his dinner guests; he disliked formal farewells, and so he kept his travel plans to himself. Since the beginning of the month he had been making lists of what to take to America and what to leave in France. He was taking his chariot, as well as Patsy's harpsichord. He had crates of books destined for his friends Washington, Franklin, and Madison. He also had plaster busts of Washington, Franklin, Lafayette, and John Paul Jones, which Jefferson had commissioned from the French sculptor Jean-Antoine Houdon; the sculptures would adorn the tea room at Monticello.[33]

He filled eighty-six crates with kitchen utensils and equipment, including a pasta-making machine from Italy. He also packed up wines, cheeses, olive oil, and Maille mustard—his favorite.[34] He crated seedlings of fruit trees and ornamental trees, including four apricots, four Cresanne pears, one white fig, two cork oaks, five larches, and three Italian poplars.[35] His preparations also included writing to James Maurice in London to request three cabins, one each for himself, Patsy, and Polly. In addition, he would require berths for James and Sally Hemings, and he wanted Sally's berth to be convenient to the girls' cabins.[36]

On September 25, Jefferson paid off the Hôtel de Langeac servants. The next day two carriages rolled up to the front door; Jefferson and his daughters climbed into a new carriage that he had just had sent over from London, while James and Sally rode inside a smaller one. Jefferson recorded in his diary that it was "a prodigiously fine day," but upon reaching the port of Le Havre, the party found the English Channel churned up by a violent storm; it took ten days before the weather cleared. Jefferson kept himself occupied by hiking through the surrounding countryside and shopping. He purchased two sheep dogs and a pregnant German shepherd that delivered two puppies before they sailed.[37]

Shortly after midnight on October 8, the Channel being calm at last, Jefferson's ship sailed for Cowes on the Isle of

Wight, where the passengers would change to an ocean-going vessel. While the group was waiting for the ship to sail, the English newspapers reported that a mob had marched on Versailles and forced the entire royal family to move to Paris. Jefferson dismissed the reports as alarmist, exaggerated, and untrustworthy—he expected a smooth transition from monarchy to democracy in France. In this optimistic mood he wrote to Maria Cosway, saying that he hoped "the ensuing spring might give us a meeting in Paris with the first swallow. So be it, my dear friend, and Adieu under the hope which springs natural out of what we wish. Once again then farewell, remember me and love me."[38] There would be no springtime rendezvous in Paris for Thomas Jefferson and Maria Cosway. The two would never see each other again.

Chapter 7

THE ART OF THE MEAL

T wo days before Christmas 1789, a carriage that was probably driven by James Hemings carried Jefferson, his two daughters, and Sally Hemings up the hill to Monticello. Gathered around the house were all of Jefferson's slaves from all of his plantations and farms. When the carriage came into sight, a large group of men and boys ran down to it, unhitched the horses, and proceeded to draw the carriage to the front door as the other slaves cheered. Martha (Patsy) described the amazing scene of their return: "Such a scene I never witnessed in my life. . . . When the door of the carriage was opened they received [my father] in their arms and bore him to the house, crowding around and kissing his hands and feet—some blubbering and crying—others laughing. It seemed impossible to satisfy their anxiety to touch and kiss the very earth which bore him."[1]

THOMAS JEFFERSON'S CRÈME BRÛLÉE

Now that the group of travelers was home, it fell to Martha, as the elder daughter, to take up the duties as mistress of Monticello. Although it is almost certain that she received advice from female relatives, and probably from some of the female house slaves as well, by and large she learned from trial and error. By the time she had daughters of her own, she was an experienced manager, ensuring that her children acquired the necessary skills to run a plantation house. In 1839, Martha's daughter Ellen Randolph Coolidge recalled that her mother had acquired her expertise through "painful conscientiousness."

After Martha's marriage to Thomas Randolph, they and their eight children moved into Monticello. Once again she was mistress of the plantation, caring for the eleven white family members as well as the sixteen slaves who lived and worked inside the house. And then there were the houseguests. Congressmen, military officers, lawyers, scientists, artists, clergymen both Protestant and Catholic, and even tourists who were complete strangers to the Jefferson family—all were made welcome at Monticello. Among the most frequent visitors were James and Dolley Madison, for whom Martha kept a room ready at all times.

Fortunately for Martha, she had the help of Burwell Colbert, Monticello's butler. He was a Hemings (Elizabeth Hemings, known as Betty, was his grandmother), the most privileged family among Jefferson's slaves. As a boy he had worked in Monticello's nail-making shop before moving on to learn the crafts of painting and window glazing. Jefferson had always thought highly of him—when Colbert was a nail maker, he was the only worker in the shop whom the overseer was forbidden to whip. When Jefferson named him as butler, Colbert took charge of Monticello's enslaved maids, waiters, and porters; naturally he reported to Martha. In addition to his duties supervising the household staff, Colbert also became Jefferson's valet, waiting on him throughout the day and attending to all of Jefferson's personal needs.

As joyful as his homecoming was, Jefferson had an important decision to make. In late September, while he and his daughters and James and Sally Hemings were at Le Havre waiting to cross the English Channel, President George Washington had named Jefferson as his secretary of state. Consequently, when Jefferson landed at Norfolk, Virginia, in late November, he discovered that just about everyone assumed he would accept the post.[2] While he was still in Paris, James Madison had written to say that a cabinet position was open if he wanted it, but Jefferson had protested that he wanted only a quiet life at Monticello.

Jefferson's biographer Joseph Ellis has observed that "incantations of virtuous retirement to rural solitude after a career of public service were familiar and even formulaic refrains within the leadership class of eighteenth-century America, none more so than within the Virginia dynasty."[3] Every American schoolboy (and the few American schoolgirls) had been taught the story of Cincinnatus, the retired general happily tending his farm, who was strong-armed into resuming his command to save Rome from its enemies. Once those enemies were crushed, Cincinnatus resigned and returned home to raise his crops. So, Jefferson's protests that he desired nothing except to bury himself in the country were almost certainly unsurprising, perhaps even expected, to others of his time.

On the trip to Monticello, four letters from Washington caught up with Jefferson, each urging him to accept the office of secretary of state. Jefferson hesitated, less from a desire for a quiet life than from genuine anxiety about the direction of Washington's government. During his first weeks back on American soil, Jefferson detected that many of his fellow citizens were inclined to place themselves under a powerful centralized government. It seemed that Washington held that position, too. Even more distressing, some Americans spoke openly about elevating their elected leader to the rank of king. The question for Jefferson became, did he want to participate in a government that appeared to be so uncongenial? It was Madison who persuaded his friend and mentor to accept Washington's offer, which Jefferson did on February 14, 1790. About five weeks later he was ferried across the Hudson River to New York City, the first capital of the United States. He rented a house on Maiden Lane, in what is known today as Lower Manhattan. Among the servants he brought with him was James Hemings. Their agreement stating that Jefferson would free James as soon as he taught French cooking to a fellow slave at Monticello was postponed—Jefferson needed a chef de cuisine for his new establishment in New York. He altered the terms of their bargain because he could—he owned James Hemings.

The U.S. Constitution called for a national capital, but did not specify a location. Northern delegates favored New York, whereas southern delegates, led by Madison, argued for a site in Virginia along the Potomac River. It was not simply a matter of regional pride—the Virginians, who had been prominent in the American Revolution, feared their influence would diminish if the government was established in a northern city. Madison argued passionately for a new city to be built along the Potomac. But northern delegates outnumbered their southern colleagues, and New York became the site of Washington's inauguration and administration. In spring 1790, southerners were still unhappy about the choice; as a compromise, there was talk of moving the government to Philadelphia.

Yet another issue, arguably more important than the location of the U.S. capital, plagued the country at this time. Each of the thirteen states was struggling to pay off the debts incurred during the American Revolution to keep their governments operational and to outfit and provision the troops they had provided to the Continental Army. The payments were crippling the states' economies, and so Alexander Hamilton, secretary of the Treasury, proposed that the federal government assume responsibility for the debts. But where Hamilton's plan liberated the states, it saddled the federal government with an $80 million obligation (approximately $1.82 billion in today's currency). To pay off the debt, the U.S. government would impose taxes on the states.

The assumption of the debts was part of Hamilton's plan to create a strong central government and weaken the sovereignty of the states. And the states knew it. Surrendering their debts to the federal government meant surrendering some of their economic autonomy as well, and no state was eager to give up its right to tend to its own affairs. As Henry Lee wrote to his fellow Virginian James Madison, "Is your love for the Constitution so ardent . . . that it should produce ruin to your native country?" By "native country," Lee meant Virginia, not America, which reveals just how local were the loyalties of the first citizens of the United States.

Early in July 1790, Jefferson was on his way to President Washington's office when he encountered Hamilton outside the building. "His look was sombre, haggard, and dejected beyond description," Jefferson wrote, "even his dress uncouth and neglected. He asked to speak with me. We stood in the street near the door. He opened the subject of the assumption of the state debts, the necessity of it in the general fiscal arrangement and it's indispensible necessity towards a preservation of the union." To Hamilton, the assumption of the states' debts appeared so essential that, he confessed to Jefferson, "if he had not credit enough to carry such a measure as that, he could be of no use, and was determined to resign."

Then Hamilton asked Jefferson to support his measure and use his influence with his southern friends to persuade them to endorse the debt assumption plan. This was an unexpected request, since Jefferson and Hamilton were often at odds.[4] Hamilton believed in a powerful national government, whereas Jefferson wanted most authority to be in the hands of the state governments. Hamilton advocated industry and technology; Jefferson dreamed of America as a nation of farmers and small tradespeople. Although Hamilton had fought in the American Revolution, in international affairs his sympathies lay with England—he admired Parliament, the fledgling factories that were springing up in English cities, the English people's devotion to law and order. And he hated revolutionary France, which he viewed as barbarous, cruel, and chaotic. Jefferson had respect for English institutions, but he could never admire a country that was ruled by a monarch. As for France, he continued to turn a blind eye to the violence of the French Revolution, preferring to see only that the monarchy had been abolished and the government was now in the hands of the people.

Jefferson put Hamilton off. He was only newly returned from France, he said, and lacked a firm grasp of the current political and economic situation in America. He conceded that "the assumption had struck me in an unfavorable light," but admitted that he was not an expert in fiscal affairs. He sympathized with Hamilton, that the measures he presented to Congress set off "the most alarming heat, the bitterest animosities" among the senators and representatives. And their sidewalk conversation ended there.[5]

Later that day, however, Jefferson sent notes to Hamilton and Madison, inviting them to dinner at his house the following day. He promised that the three of them would be alone. He hoped that among themselves they would "find some temperament for the present fever." Jefferson had faith that "men of sound heads and honest views needed nothing more than explanation and mutual understanding to enable them to unite in some measures which might enable us to get along."[6]

Madison and Hamilton accepted, and, as Jefferson had promised, the three of them dined alone.

Author Charles A. Cerami, working closely with the research staff at Monticello, has created a likely menu for this momentous dinner, drawing each course from dishes that Jefferson enjoyed whether he was dining with family or with guests. The green salad came with a wine jelly made by boiling calves' feet until it became a gelatinous mass; then milk, lemon juice, sugar, and Madeira wine were added. Next served was capon, a common dish in Virginia, but improved thanks to James Hemings's training in France. The bird arrived at the table stuffed with truffles, artichoke bottoms, chestnut puree, and Virginia ham and was served with a sauce of Calvados, the apple brandy of Normandy. This was followed by *boeuf à la mode*, a top round of beef with onions, carrots, bacon, sprigs of parsley and thyme, and a veal knuckle bone, all cooked slowly in a Dutch oven for four to five hours. Then came small plates of confections, such as macaroons and meringues. Dessert was vanilla ice cream stuffed inside a warm puff pastry. Jefferson served a different wine for each course: Hermitage, his favorite white wine, as an aperitif; a white Bordeaux with the salad; Montepulciano with the capon; Chambertin, one of the finest wines in his cellar, with the beef; and Champagne with the sweets.[7]

Whatever the actual menu may have been, James's cuisine and Jefferson's wine put all three men in an amiable, reasonable, let's-get-things-done frame of mind. By the end of the evening, Madison agreed not to oppose the debt assumption bill when it came before Congress, although he would not vote in favor of it. Jefferson suggested that "as the pill would be a bitter one to the Southern states, something should be done to soothe them." The "something" he had in mind was moving the national capital to a site on the "Patowmac," as he spelled it.[8] Hamilton agreed. While a site was being selected and the new city planned, the government would relocate temporarily to Philadelphia. So ended one of the most momentous private dinners in American history, and it had been prepared by James Hemings.

The assumption bill passed in Congress, and in December

1790 the government moved to Philadelphia, where it would remain for the next decade while the city of Washington was designed and a capitol for Congress and the Supreme Court, as well as a residence for the president, were built. As for the truce between Jefferson and Hamilton, it did not last long. In 1792 the two political opponents took to attacking each other in the press. Hamilton and his allies, writing under aliases such as "Catullus" and "Scourge," accused Jefferson of dabbling in "political mystery and deception." Jefferson fired back through his ally, newspaper publisher Philip Freneau, who labeled Hamilton and his supporters "monarchists . . . tories . . . anti-republicans . . . monocrats."[9]

Although he was fighting back, Jefferson felt that Hamilton was getting the upper hand, that the latter's slurs were more effective than his own. In a letter to President Washington, Jefferson complained, saying, "I will not suffer my retirement to be clouded by the slanders of a man whose history, from the moment at which history can stoop to notice him, is a tissue of machinations against the liberty of the country which has not only received and given him bread, but heaped it's honors on his head."[10]

In an attempt to drive Hamilton out of the cabinet, Jefferson wrote a list of charges accusing the secretary of the Treasury of mismanaging government funds, manipulating the markets, and even embezzling money from the very federal department he was entrusted to manage. Jefferson drafted his accusations as a speech, which his political ally, Representative William Branch Giles, delivered in the House of Representatives on February 27, 1793. Jefferson and his friends assumed Hamilton would be so ashamed that he would resign from office. Instead, two days later, Hamilton published a reply exposing the charges against him as deliberately invented and completely false.[11]

It was Jefferson who resigned. In the fall of 1793, he left Philadelphia and headed home to Monticello. James Hemings was still with him. Compelled to serve as Jefferson's chef, first in New York and then in Philadelphia, he'd had no opportunity to train his successor. He had been back in America for nearly four years, and it appears he was becoming impatient and may have expressed his discontent to his master, because among Jefferson's papers is a contract between the two men, drawn up before they left Philadelphia:

> *Having been at great expence in having James Hemings taught the art of cookery, desiring to befriend him, and to require from him as little in return as possible, I do hereby promise and declare, that if the said James shall go with me to Monticello in the course of the ensuing winter, when I go to reside there myself, and shall there continue until he shall have taught such person as I shall place under him for that purpose to be a good cook, this previous condition being performed,*

> *he shall be thereupon made free, and I will there-*
> *upon execute all proper instruments to make him*
> *free. Given under my hand and seal in the county*
> *of Philadelphia and state of Pennsylvania this*
> *15th. day of September one thousand seven hun-*
> *dred and ninety three.*[12]

At Monticello Jefferson chose twenty-three-year-old Peter Hemings, James's younger brother, to master the art of French cooking. For more than two years, James and Peter worked side by side in the basement kitchen below Monticello's south pavillion.[13] All the kitchen equipment and utensils acquired in France were now installed in the house. In 1796 Jefferson had a charcoal-burning brick stove built along one wall of the kitchen; this appliance eliminated much of the need for open-fire cooking. Now it was easier, not to mention safer, for James and Peter to sauté meat and vegetables or let soups and stews simmer. The stove had eight openings or grates, which generated a great deal of heat, so Jefferson had the stove placed below a window, for ventilation. At one end of the stove stood a large copper kettle that provided hot water.[14]

As mistress of Monticello, Jefferson's daughter Martha planned the daily menus that the Hemings brothers and their assistants would prepare. According to Isaac Jefferson, the master of the house "never went into the kitchen except to wind up the clock."[15]

To get the food to the table, the kitchen staff used covered platters that had a compartment filled with hot water or hot sand to keep the food warm. The platters were carried into the house, to the office, where more servants transferred the cooked food to porcelain or silver serving dishes. These were placed inside a revolving cabinet; when the servants turned the cabinet, the serving dishes appeared in the adjoining dining room. There, Jefferson's butler Martin Hemings (he would be succeeded by Hemings's nephew Burwell Colbert) carried the covered dishes to the small tables that stood between each guest—Jefferson had kept the habit he had acquired in France of letting guests help themselves. Meanwhile, a servant in the wine cellar sent up bottles to the dining room by means of a dumbwaiter.[16]

Isaac Jefferson tells us that Jefferson "never would have less than eight covers at dinner—if nobody at table but himself." If he had guests, Jefferson "had from eight to thirty-two covers for dinner: plenty of wine, best old Antigua rum and cider."[17] Peter Fossett, son of Edith Fossett, who succeeded the Hemings brothers as chef at Monticello, recalled that so many visitors came to the house that life at Monticello was "a merry go round of hospitalities."[18]

After more than two years of intense training, in early 1795 Peter Hemings was ready to take over as chef of Monticello. The day of James's emancipation came at last on February 5, 1796. In the presence of two witnesses, Jefferson wrote the necessary document that made James a free man:

*This indenture made at Monticello in the
county of Albemarle and commonwealth of Virginia on the fifth day of February one thousand
seven hundred and ninety six witnesseth that I
Thomas Jefferson of Monticello aforesaid do
emancipate, manumit and make free James
Hemings, son of Betty Hemings, which said
James is now of the age of thirty years so that
in future he shall be free and of free condition,
and discharged of all duties and claims of servitude whatsoever, and shall have all the rights
and privileges of a freedman. In witness
whereof I have hereto set my hand and seal on
the day and year above written, and have made
these presents double of the same date, tenor
and indenture one whereof is lodged in the
court of Albemarle aforesaid to be recorded, and
the other is delivered by me to the said James
Hemings to be produced when and where it
may be necessary.*[19]

Before he left Monticello, James wrote an inventory of the kitchen equipment. In addition to the many French copper pots and pans, he also mentions brass and marble "pistle[s] & mortar[s]"; most likely these came from France, too, where they were standard equipment in any kitchen.[20] Then with thirty dollars in his pocket, James set out for Philadelphia,

This indenture made at Monticello in the county of Albemarle & commonwealth of Virginia on the fifth day of February one thousand seven hundred and ninety six witnesseth that I Thomas Jefferson of Monticello aforesaid do emancipate manumit & make free James Hemings, son of Betty Hemings, which said James is now of the age of thirty years so that in future he shall be free and of free condition, & discharged of all duties & claims of servitude whatsoever, & shall have all the rights and privileges of a freedman. In witness whereof I have hereto set my hand & seal on the day & year abovewritten, and have made these presents double of the same date, tenor & indenture one whereof is lodged in the court of Albemarle aforesaid to be recorded, & the other is delivered by me to the said James Hemings to be produced when & where it may be necessary.

Signed, sealed & delivered
in presence of

John Carr

Francis Anderson

Thomas Jefferson's deed of manumission to James Hemings, dated February 5, 1796. (Courtesy Special Collections, University of Virginia Library, Charlottesville, Va., accession #5589) where he found work as a cook. There is some evidence that he went back to France for a time. In 1797 he was back in Philadelphia and got in touch with Jefferson, telling him that on his next trip to Europe he planned to visit Spain.[21]

In 1801, when Jefferson was the newly elected president, he sent an intermediary to invite James to serve as chef at the President's House (not yet called the White House). James was working as a cook at a tavern in Baltimore and sent back the reply that he would like to receive a few lines from Jefferson about the post; Jefferson never sent the note and hired another man as chef.

As president, Jefferson continued his merry-go-round of hospitalities. His predecessor, John Adams, grumbled, "I dined a large company once or twice a week, Jefferson dined a dozen every day. I held levees once a week. Jefferson's whole eight years was a levee."[22] In fact, Jefferson abandoned the levee tradition established by Washington and Adams—these afternoon receptions, which originated with the kings of England, were too aristocratic for a good democrat like Jefferson. He did enjoy dinner parties, however, and to keep them egalitarian he seated his guests at a round table. These were not mere social gatherings; as he had learned in France and confirmed at the dinner with Hamilton and Madison, fine food and fine wine combined with lively conversation could serve a political purpose. Historian James S. Young characterized these dinner parties as one of Jefferson's "power techniques" for reconciling political opponents and advancing his own political agenda.[23]

Federalist congressman William J. Plumer of New Hampshire joined eleven other members of Congress at a one such dinner party. In a letter home to his wife, he praised the president for serving "a very good dinner, with a profusion of fruits and sweetmeats. The wine was the best I ever drank, particularly the champagne, which was indeed delicious."[24] After dining with the president, the Reverend Manasseh Cutler of Ohio wrote to his wife of the lavish meal Jefferson served, including a dish that was new to him—"a pie called macaroni."[25] Most likely this was the dish we know today as mac and cheese.

Days before his inauguration as president, Jefferson wrote to the French envoy, Philippe de Letombe, asking for advice on finding a French chef and a French maître d'hôtel. Letombe found the men Jefferson needed: Joseph Rapin, a gentlemanly Frenchman, and Honoré Julien, who had been the chef for George Washington during the last four months of his presidency. Jefferson was pleased with both, but after six months, Rapin moved on. He was replaced by yet another Frenchman, Étienne Lemaire, lately maître d'hôtel in the home of the wealthy Bingham family of Philadelphia.[26]

No doubt, Jefferson gave Lemaire the same instructions as he once sent to Rapin. "While I wish to have every thing good in it's kind, and handsome in stile, I am a great enemy to waste and useless extravagance, and see them with real pain."[27]

The result was what Washington hostess Margaret Bayard Smith described as "republican simplicity . . . united to Epicurean delicacy."[28] As he had done with James, Jefferson brought two slaves from Monticello to learn French cuisine from Chef Julien. Edith Fossett was fifteen years old when she began her apprenticeship, and her sister Fanny Hern was eighteen. They would become the French chefs during Jefferson's final years.[29]

Like Jefferson, Lemaire kept an account book, which has survived. In it, we can see what he purchased in the Washington, D.C., markets for the president's table. And as one would expect, Jefferson and his guests ate exceptionally well. Turkey was served at least once, and more often twice, a week. Pheasant, quail, pigeon, and canvasback ducks also made regular appearances, although Jefferson's favorite game bird was the guinea hen. Fish was cheap because it was readily available—rockfish and sturgeon weighing fifty pounds or more were pulled straight from the Potomac River, while the Chesapeake Bay yielded up an endless supply of oysters, which were sold two for a penny, or ninety cents for a gallon. The president, his staff, and his guests ate so much bread that the cooks could not meet the demand. Additional amounts were purchased from a Washington baker named Peter Miller, who, in a typical month, delivered $50 worth of bread and rolls to the President's House. Dairy products were pricey: milk was nine cents a quart, butter thirty cents a pound, eggs twenty cents a dozen. Each month, Lemaire spent between $500 and $600 on food, sometimes laying out as much as $50 in one day.

As president, Jefferson received an annual salary of $25,000 per year. He thus was able to supplement the President's House provisions with his favorite luxury goods, paying out of his own pocket for European wines and delicacies. But the building had no wine cellar, and no part of the basement was cool enough to store the bottles properly, so Jefferson had a cellar dug on the grounds. In addition to wine, he ordered from Europe olive oil, anchovies, and Parmesan cheese—all new taste sensations to his guests.[30]

In politics and in his personal life, Thomas Jefferson was a complicated man, but in one thing he was consistent: he wanted the best of everything, for himself and for his country. He loved what was native to America—Indian corn, Virginia ham, representative government—but he knew there was more to be had. And so when he went to Europe, he traveled with his eyes and his mind wide open, and his taste buds eager for the next delicacy. Like a true tourist, Jefferson could not wait to bring the treasures he found back to the United States, hence all those crates of mustard, and nectarines, and almonds, and olive oil, not to mention the 680 bottles of wine.[31] Patrick Henry, that culinary chauvinist, denounced Jefferson's newly acquired European palate: "He has abjured his native victuals in favor of French cuisine." Like most charges that political opponents hurl at one another, this one is untrue. Jefferson didn't abandon his native victuals; he married them to those from France.

The man who made that possible was James Hemings. In a three-year apprenticeship in Paris, he mastered French cuisine as well as the French language. When he took over as chef de cuisine at Jefferson's house in Paris, the meals he prepared must have met the highest French standards, because Jefferson did not hesitate to send dinner invitations to some of the most distinguished and discriminating men and women in France. And, of course, it was James's cuisine that put those determined rivals, Alexander Hamilton, James Madison, and Thomas Jefferson, in the mood for some serious political horse trading.

In summer 1801, James returned to Monticello to serve as chef during Jefferson's long vacation from Washington. In September, when Jefferson arrived home from the capital, James returned to Baltimore. A month later, Jefferson received the tragic news that James Hemings had killed himself. He had been drinking heavily for several days, and while delirious with alcohol he committed suicide. He was thirty-six years old. Jefferson wrote to his chief builder at Monticello and asked him to deliver the unhappy news to the Hemings family in person.[32]

*   *   *

Thanks to his training in France, James Hemings founded a culinary dynasty in America. His brother and successor, Peter, preserved James's recipes and taught them, as well as his techniques, to other slaves at Monticello, including Edith Fossett. She then passed these skills on to her son Peter Fossett (James Hemings's great-nephew). In 1850, after Peter Fossett's family and friends purchased his freedom, he moved to Cincinnati, where he opened a catering business and went on to become one of the most successful caterers in the city.

Jefferson longed for "choice meals," as he called them, and it was James Hemings who fulfilled that longing. The master-and-slave relationship was surely fraught with tensions and resentments that today we can only imagine. Yet it is apparent there existed some friendly feelings, perhaps even affection, that linked these two men. Indeed, after his emancipation, James stayed in touch with Jefferson. He spent some of the final months of his life back in the Monticello kitchen, among family and friends. When word of James's "tragical end" reached Jefferson, he sent a friend to Baltimore to learn what had happened, and then he arranged for the news to be broken to the Hemings family as gently as possible.

It is unfortunate we do not know more about James Hemings. It is a loss to culinary history that more of his recipes have not survived. And it is tragic that a man with such a gift would become an alcoholic and take his own life. His cooking set the standard for Jefferson; for the rest of his life, he would have either a French chef or a slave who had been trained in the art of French cuisine to serve in his kitchen.

Thomas Jefferson's Crème Brûlée

In 1802 Mahlon Dickerson, a Philadelphia judge, dined at the President's House. It must have been a memorable meal, because Dickerson wrote afterward that Jefferson "takes good care of his table. No man in America keeps a better."[33] It is the type of compliment that Thomas Jefferson and James Hemings would have savored.

EPILOGUE

Thomas Jefferson served two terms as president of the United States. In 1809 he was succeeded in the White House by his friend James Madison. Jefferson went home to Monticello and never again visited Washington, D.C. In 1814, after an invading British army burned the Library of Congress, Jefferson offered to sell his personal library to the federal government. The following year, Congress approved an appropriation of $23,950 for the purchase of his collection of 6,487 books. No sooner had the cases been shipped off to Washington than Jefferson resumed buying books. At age seventy-six, Jefferson founded the University of Virginia. He designed the curriculum, recruited the faculty, and served as the first rector, or president. The school opened in 1819 with eight professors and sixty-eight students. Today it has almost eight thousand full-time faculty and more than twenty-one thousand students.

On July 4, 1826, as the citizens of the United States celebrated the fiftieth anniversary of the signing of the Declaration of Independence, Thomas Jefferson and John Adams both lay dying. Adams's last words were, "Thomas Jefferson still lives." He was mistaken: his friend had died just hours earlier.

Jefferson's daughter Martha married her third cousin, Thomas Mann Randolph, in 1790. The couple had eleven children, yet their marriage was hardly a success. For many years, Martha and her children lived with her father at Monticello and in Washington, D.C., where Martha acted as hostess at the President's House. To settle debts left after Jefferson's death, the family was forced to sell Monticello. Martha spent the rest of her life living with one or another of her children. She died in 1836 and is buried in the Jefferson family cemetery at Monticello.

Upon her return to America, Polly Jefferson took to calling herself Maria. In 1797 she married John Eppes, one of the cousins she had played with as a child. They lived at Eppington and had two children, a son and a daughter. In 1804, two months after giving birth to a girl, Maria died.

It is generally accepted by scholars that Sally Hemings became Jefferson's mistress and together they had six children, four of whom survived to adulthood. Jefferson did not free Sally while he was alive nor in his will. It seems that Martha Jefferson Randolph freed her, although the exact date of her manumission is unknown. Sally spent her final years in Charlottesville, living with her sons Madison and Easton. She died in 1835.

Many of Jefferson's friends and dinner guests from his Paris years fell victim to the French Revolution. In 1794 Princess Lubomirski was beheaded. For the crime of defending Louis XVI at his trial, Chrétien-Guillaume de Lamoignon de Malesherbes was forced to watch as his daughter, son-in-law, and granddaughter were beheaded; then he, too, was taken to the guillotine. The Marquis de Condorcet may have been a champion of liberty and human rights, but in the eyes of the revolutionary tribunal, his noble blood outweighed his political principles. Rather than face public execution, he drank poison. The Duke de la Rochefoucauld-Liancourt escaped France in 1793; he forced a Norman fisherman, at gunpoint, to take him across the English Channel. Antoine Lavoisier would pay for his association with the tax system: on May 8, 1794, he was guillotined in Paris. Before the French Revolution was over, all his fellow tax collectors would lose their heads as well. As for Jefferson's old flame, Maria Cosway moved to Lodi, Italy, where she became the benefactress of a convent school for girls. She and Jefferson corresponded from time to time; her last letter to him arrived a year before his death. In her home, Cosway kept a portrait of her friend, painted by John Trumbull. In 1976, for the bicentennial of the United States, the government of Italy presented the portrait to President Gerald Ford. Today the painting hangs in the White House.

When Jefferson left Washington in 1809, he became so

overwrought saying good-bye to his maître d'hôtel, Étienne Lemaire, that all he could manage was a brief "adieu." Later he wrote to Lemaire, whom he praised as a "faithful, & skillful" steward. He added that Lemaire's "whole conduct [was] so marked with good humour, industry, sobriety & economy as never to have given me one moment's dissatisfaction." Lemaire moved to Philadelphia soon after leaving the President's House. In 1817, a friend to whom he had loaned $5,000 went bankrupt. Despondent at the loss, Lemaire threw himself into the Schuylkill River and drowned.

Chef Honoré Julien remained in Washington, where he opened a small shop that sold pastries, candy, and ice cream; he also managed a catering business. He kept in touch with Jefferson and occasionally sent him gourmet gifts, such as Swiss cheese or canvasback ducks. He died in 1830. His son Auguste, whom he had trained as a chef, often catered banquets at the White House during the administration of President James K. Polk.

At Jefferson's table at Monticello, politicians and members of Washington society, as well as myriad visitors to the plantation, were exposed to fine French cuisine. Yet, despite this pocket of culinary adventurousness, Americans of all classes held fast to the style of cooking common in the British Isles. In fact, Americans generally became suspicious—even hostile—when confronted with what they viewed as "fancified" food. Moreover, by the 1830s a large majority of Americans had begun to see their plain food as a virtue. Cookbooks emphasized simplicity and frugality, not meals that brought a succession of interesting flavors to the table. Plain cuisine even became an issue in the presidential campaign of 1836: William Henry Harrison's supporters managed to convince voters that their man was just ordinary folks, content to live in a log cabin, eat his corn mush, and wash it down with old-fashioned hard cider. Martin Van Buren, his opponent, was portrayed as a foppish, Frenchified, un-American snob who sipped Champagne from a silver goblet and liked to begin his meals with consommé. The smear worked, and the gourmandizing Van Buren lost the election. It was not until the late nineteenth century, when the new American millionaires began importing French chefs to serve in their kitchens, that French cuisine truly gained ground in the United States.

In the twentieth century, Americans came to consider the cuisine of France as the epitome of fine dining, something reserved for master chefs working in multistar restaurants. Then, in 1961, Julia Child published *Mastering the Art of French Cooking*, a three-pound tome that demystified complicated cooking techniques and made French cuisine accessible to home cooks everywhere. It was a groundbreaking achievement. Child's cookbook remained on the best-seller list for five years and inspired four televised cooking shows as well as a hit film, 2009's *Julie and Julia*. Child was so successful and so popular that she is widely believed to be responsible for single-handedly introducing Americans to French food. That is a misconception, of course; the real credit goes to a founding father and one of his slaves.

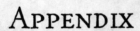

APPENDIX

THE WINE
CONNOISSEUR

Wine lovers like to quote Thomas Jefferson, who once described the drink as "a necessary of life." It is a fine phrase, but the editors of the *Thomas Jefferson Encyclopedia* point out that their subject considered many things a necessity, including books, salad oil, salt, and hair powder.[1] Jefferson was introduced to wine in Williamsburg at the dinner tables of his mentor George Wythe and the governor of Virginia, Francis Farquier. He learned to love it while in Paris, and he immersed himself in the art of winemaking on his tour through the vineyards of France and northern Italy. Jefferson's experiences in Europe made him eager to introduce the great wines of the Old World to the inhabitants of the New World.

Jefferson was not always a wine connoisseur. A 1769 inventory from Shadwell, his childhood home, reveals that the family's cellar held 4 bottles of Portuguese wine, 15 bottles of

Madeira, 54 bottles of cider, and 83 bottles of rum. But his tastes evolved. Another inventory dated 1772—the year he married Martha Wayles Skelton—lists 10 bottles of port, 29 bottles of beer, 31 bottles of miscellaneous wines, 37 bottles of Portuguese wine, 72 bottles of Madeira, 3 gallons of rum, and half a hogshead (the equivalent of 27½ gallons) of Madeira.[2]

The man who was most influential in Jefferson's oenological education was Philip Mazzei, an Italian surgeon, merchant, and horticulturalist with an interest in human rights. In 1773 he sailed to America to meet the people who had such a strong sense of independence. Like Jefferson, Mazzei studied new agricultural methods that would increase crop yields. The two men met not long after Mazzei landed in Virginia, and it appears each recognized in the other a kindred soul. Early one morning, the pair hiked the land adjacent to Monticello looking for a suitable tract for Mazzei's farm. They found four hundred acres east of Jefferson's estate that had exactly the type of soil Mazzei was looking for: a mixture of clay and pebbles such as one finds in the French wine region of Burgundy. Mazzei bought the land and called the farm Colle, Italian for "The Hill."[3]

From Europe Mazzei had brought ten Italian vignerons (winemakers) as well as vines, olive saplings, and silkworm eggs. He intended to introduce three things to America that the country did not yet have: a vineyard, an olive grove, and a silk industry. Soon after acquiring the property, Mazzei announced his "Proposal for forming a Company or Partnership, for the Purpose of raising and making Wine, Oil, agruminous Plants, and Silk." Jefferson became a partner in what was known as "the Wine Company." Other investors signed on, inspired by Mazzei's assurances that no spot in America was "better calculated" to be America's wine country than Virginia.[4]

In 1774 a frost killed all the grapevines but did not dampen Mazzei's enthusiasm for his new home. When the wine, olive oil, and silk project failed, he took up a new interest—America's struggle for independence from England—and enlisted in the Albemarle County militia. When Jefferson had worked up a rough draft of the Declaration of Independence, he showed it first to Mazzei and asked for his opinion. Mazzei became a Virginia citizen, and in 1778 the government of Virginia sent him to Italy to secure funds for the revolution from the grand duke of Tuscany.[5]

Jefferson's wine education began in Williamsburg, after he had graduated from the College of William and Mary and while he was studying law under the direction of George Wythe. Wythe had a wine cellar, as did Governor Farquier. The wines Jefferson likely drank most often were claret from France's Bordeaux region and Madeira, a fortified wine like port, which came from Portugal's Madeira Islands. At the time, these wines were popular among gentlemen both in America and in England. Jefferson especially enjoyed Madeira, and it was the wine the Continental Congress called for to toast the adoption of the Declaration of Independence.[6]

Even before he traveled to France in 1784, Jefferson's palate inclined toward French wines. In France he discovered Champagne and Chambertin, a grand cru vineyard, which became one of his favorite wines. (By the way, *grand cru* identifies a vineyard that has the highest potential to make great wines; it is not a guarantee that every vintage will be stellar.) He also liked wines from Italy and southern France, and it appears that he never lost his taste for inexpensive Portuguese wines. Among his favorite Italian wines were Montepulciano—virtually unknown to American wine lovers in Jefferson's day—as well as Chianti, Marsala, and the sweet dessert wine the Italians call Vin Santo, because many priests choose this as the wine they consecrated at Mass. His cellar also held wines from Spain, Germany, Hungary, and even Greece. When Daniel Webster came to dinner at Monticello, Jefferson produced a bottle Webster called "Samian," which wine historian John Hailman believes was the Muscat produced on the Greek island of Samos.[7]

In French wine, Jefferson demanded the best: Château d'Yquem, Château Margaux, Latour, Lafite, and Haut-Brion. These are wines that connoisseurs still revere. He ordered cases of Champagne and served it at virtually every dinner he hosted in the President's House. For most of his guests, this was their introduction to sparkling wine. It has been said that by serving Champagne to distinguished men and women from every corner of America, Jefferson single-handedly made the drink popular, a favored wine for festive occasions.[8]

Most of his wines Jefferson imported directly from Europe, but that was no guarantee of quality. Extremes of heat or cold during the crossings damaged the wine. Some ships bearing his orders sank in storms or fell victim to pirates. Just as bad as "the lawless rovers of the sea" were the dishonest carriers who loaded the wine casks aboard small boats and sailed them up the Potomac or the James River to Jefferson. Occasionally, some "rascally boatmen," as Jefferson called them, helped themselves to the contents, refilling the casks with water.[9]

Jefferson enjoyed wine the way he enjoyed fine food—it was something that gave him pleasure, it was something he could share with guests, it was something he could study. In his enthusiasm, at his President's House dinners Jefferson often discussed the wines that were being served that evening. Perhaps he went on too long, perhaps it was a one-sided conversation since so few people in American could hold their own against Jefferson in a discussion about wine. At least one guest, John Quincy Adams, found Jefferson's wine talk tedious and "not very edifying."

For a wine lover, he drank abstemiously, three or four glasses at dinner, never more. And wineglasses in Jefferson's day were small, holding perhaps a third of the amount of a modern balloon wineglass. As a rule he drank modest wines, what we would call the house wine, when he was dining with his family, and saved the fine wines for guests. To the house wine,

This shipping bill dated September 27, 1821, "by order, for account & risk of Thomas Jefferson Esq. of Monticello (Virginia)," details a large shipment of foodstuffs bound for the port of Boston. Packed inside cases were hundreds of bottles of red and white wine, including "white wine of Limoux" and "Muscat de Rivesaltes," as well as superfine olive oil, macaroni, and anchovies. (Courtesy Library of Congress, Manuscript Division, Thomas Jefferson Papers) he usually added a little water, perhaps to cut the alcohol or smooth out the flavor of a rough wine. In a letter to Joseph Fenwick, the American consul in Bordeaux, Jefferson placed an order for himself and for George Washington: ten dozen bottles of Château d'Yquem for himself, thirty dozen for Washington; ten dozen bottles of Château Rausan for himself and twenty dozen bottles of Château Latour for Washington. He also asked Fenwick, "I must beg you to add 10 dozen for me of a good white vin ordinaire, or indeed something better, that is to say of such a quality as will do to mix with water, and also be drinkable alone."[10]

After having studied the architecture of Palladio, Jefferson decided to build a new house in the Palladian style atop his little mountain. When he tasted French cuisine, he decided to have James Hemings trained as a French chef. His encounters with macaroni convinced him that he must have a pasta-making machine at Monticello. As much as possible, whatever good things he found, Jefferson wanted to be able to make them at home. Such is the case with wine. In spite of the failure of the Mazzei Wine Company, Jefferson still hoped that wine could be made in Virginia. He even planted cork trees so that the stoppers would be on hand when he bottled his first vintage.

Jefferson had two vineyards laid out beside his garden wall, one measuring nine thousand square feet, the other measuring sixteen thousand square feet. He had cuttings for twenty-four different varieties of grapes sent to him from Europe, and in 1807 his slaves planted 287 vines. Like Mazzei, he planted *Vitis vinifera*, the cornerstone of European vineyards. That species could not thrive in America, where it fell prey to black rot and phylloxera, two diseases that are fatal to wine vines. When that experiment failed, Jefferson tried to make wine from native American grapes, such as the fox grape, *V. labrusca*, and the Scuppernong, *V. rotundifolia*. The vines were pest-resistant, but the wines they produced were unpalatable.[11]

The War of 1812 cut off Jefferson from his suppliers in Europe. In 1815, he lamented to a wine merchant in Norfolk that the war with England "at length left me without a drop of wine." To refill his depleted cellar, he wrote to Stephan Cathalan, an American residing in Marseille, who arranged for shipments to Monticello. "I resume our old correspondence with a declaration of wants," Jefferson said. He wanted Hermitage, a red Roussillon, and a certain red wine from Nice that Cathalan had been able to purchase for him before the war.[12]

And so Jefferson began to fill his cellar once again. Sometimes, a shipment of five hundred bottles would arrive in a single day. All were locked in the cellar, behind a door of double thickness, in a room where all the windows were barred. Wine was something Thomas Jefferson could not live without. Even in his final years, when he was deeply in debt, he continued to purchase it. At his death, there were six hundred bottles of wine in the Monticello cellar.

VEGETABLES:
THOMAS JEFFERSON'S
"PRINCIPAL DIET"

Vegetables were Thomas Jefferson's favorite food. He did eat meat, however, so we cannot call him a vegetarian. By the standards of his day, his preference for vegetables was surprising: in eighteenth-century America, meat was just about everyone's preferred dish, and vegetables were often regarded as a garnish. "I have lived temperately," he wrote to a physician in 1819, "eating little animal food, and that not as an aliment, so much as a condiment for the vegetables which constitute my principal diet."[1] His granddaughter Ellen W. Coolidge recalled that "he lived principally on vegetables."[2] After dining with Jefferson, Daniel Webster observed, "He enjoys his dinner well, taking with meat a large proportion of vegetables."[3] And Jefferson's overseer, Edmund Bacon, tells us that when Jefferson did eat meat, he was "especially fond of

Guinea fowls," although he would also eat "good beef, mutton, and lambs." Unlike most Americans of the period, "He never [ate] much hog meat."[4]

In his thousand-foot-long vegetable garden, Jefferson grew almost all the vegetables, fruits, and herbs he needed to feed himself, his family, and their guests. Over a period of nearly sixty years he experimented with ninety-nine species of vegetables and three hundred thirty varieties. He also cultivated plants that were unknown in his neighbors' gardens, including tomatoes, peppers, eggplant, and peanuts.[5]

Jefferson's decision to plant a large vegetable, fruit, and herb garden was as practical as it was botanical. There was no large-scale produce market in Albemarle County. Like his neighbors, if he wanted choice fruit and vegetables, he had to grow his own. Of course, Jefferson could not simply buy some seedlings, stick them in the ground, and then walk away to let time and nature do their work. He had to cultivate and maintain the beds carefully. He recorded which varieties he acquired, the characteristics of each plant, the manner in which they were planted, how they thrived, and the date they were harvested and served to him at dinner. A true gardener, he loved watching his plants grow and savored the foods they produced, but he also relished keeping detailed statistics about each crop. He once wrote, "There is not a shoot of grass that springs uninteresting to me."[6]

The scientist in Jefferson made of his garden an outdoor

laboratory. He conducted "experiments" with plants not only to determine their viability but also to find the hardiest, best-producing varieties for the local climate and conditions. He imported a type of broccoli from Italy and planted a fig tree he had acquired in France. He raised beans that Lewis and Clark had found on their expedition through the American West. "I am curious to select one or two of the best species or variety of every garden vegetable," he wrote, "and to reject all others from the garden to avoid the dangers of mixing or degeneracy."

The man who built one of the most beautiful homes in eighteenth-century America also desired his garden to be visually appealing. Along the border of the square in which he grew tomatoes, for example, he planted okra and sesame plants. The smooth, red skin of the tomatoes contrasted with the rough, deep green of the okra, while the sesame plant, standing five or six feet tall, added height and visual interest. When he planted eggplant, he alternated white and purple varieties. The cherry trees he placed along the walkway through the garden, where they would provide shade.[7]

Within the garden stood a small brick pavilion designed by Jefferson. It was perfectly square, measuring thirteen feet six inches on each side. Also on all four sides was a tall arched window, so that the interior was flooded with light and would catch passing breezes in summer. In this little building Jefferson liked to read or sit quietly and enjoy the view of his garden. Not long after his death in 1826, a violent storm blew down the structure. Archaeologists uncovered its foundations in 1980, and the pavilion has since been reconstructed.[8]

Jefferson probably directed most of the work in the garden, with his enslaved field hands doing all the planting, weeding, hoeing, and harvesting. However, he was not above getting his own hands dirty. From the recollections of his slave Isaac Jefferson, we learn that, "for amusement he [Jefferson] would work sometimes in the garden for half an hour in right good earnest in the cool of the evening."

In 1794 Jefferson hired Robert Bailey to design Monticello's gardens and assigned Wormley Hughes, one of his most trusted slaves, to be Bailey's assistant. By 1806 Hughes was principal gardener. He tended the seedlings in the nursery, planted the flowers, manured the soil and tended the vegetable garden, and installed the new plants Jefferson sent from Washington. Jefferson routinely sent instructions to his overseer about what gardening or landscaping work Wormley must do: "He must plant the Pitch pine in the woods along the new road leading from the house to the river, on both sides of the road."[9] Years later, Ellen Coolidge would recall watching her grandfather and Wormley lay out the flower gardens, Wormley armed with a hoe and a shovel and Jefferson with a measuring line to ensure the geometric precision of the beds.[10]

In an era before chemical pesticides, insects could cause serious damage to plants both cultivated and wild. That is exactly what happened to the Monticello garden in 1793, and

Martha Jefferson Randolph had to report the unhappy news to her father. Ever the seeker of scientific solutions, he wrote back: "We will try this winter to cover our garden with a heavy coating of manure. When earth is rich it bids defiance to droughts, yields in abundance, and of the best quality. I suspect that the insects which have harassed you have been encouraged by the feebleness of your plants; and that has been produced by the lean state of the soil."[11]

Jefferson could be very enthusiastic about a particular variety of fruit or vegetable. He once declared that the Marseille fig was "incomparably the finest fig I have ever seen," and on another occasion he praised the flowering acacia as "the most delicious flowering shrub in the world."[12] Peter J. Hatch, director of the gardens and grounds at Monticello, believes it is likely that Jefferson's favorite vegetable was the English or spring pea: three of the twenty-four squares in his extensive garden were devoted exclusively to peas, and over the years he experimented with twenty-three varieties.[13] Some of these Jefferson acquired from Bernard McMahon of Philadelphia, a botanist and arguably America's best-informed nurseryman. His 648-page book *The American Gardener's Calendar*, with its step-by-step instructions on how to plant and care for just about every vegetable and flower available in the United States, became Jefferson's horticultural bible. Jefferson thought so highly of the man that when Lewis and Clark returned from the Louisiana Territory with more than 170 plant specimens, he chose McMahon to catalogue them.[14]

Given its temperate climate and rich soil, Virginia was home to many serious gardeners and farmers. There was a local custom at the time to hold a friendly competition: whoever was first to harvest English peas had to throw a pea dinner for fellow gardeners. Jefferson was a frequent competitor, and the presence in his garden of the Hotspur variety of spring peas—renowned for its quick growth—suggests that he wanted to win. Usually, a neighbor named Divers was victor of the pea-growing contest; only once was Jefferson's crop the first to come in, but he kept the news quiet. When his family wanted to announce his success, he asked them not to. "Say nothing about it," he instructed, "it will be more agreeable to our friend [Divers] to think that he never fails."[15]

If English peas were Jefferson's favorite vegetable, the runner-up was probably lettuce. Étienne Lemaire, Jefferson's maître d'hôtel during the years when he was president, kept meticulous records of his purchases in the markets of Washington and Georgetown. In 1806, Lemaire bought lettuce ninety times. At Monticello, Jefferson grew eight varieties, each of which had a different planting and harvesting date; in this way, he could have fresh lettuce from summer into early winter. One of his relatives, Mary Randolph, tells us that slaves picked lettuce early in the morning, then plunged the leaves into a cold-water bath to keep them fresh until dinner, which was usually served at four in the afternoon. She also included the salad dressing recipe made at Monticello: oil, white or tarragon vinegar, sliced hard-boiled eggs, salt, powdered sugar, and mustard, garnished with sliced scallions.[16] Rarely was the oil for Jefferson's salad dressing made from olives—importing it from Europe was expensive. Jefferson felt the loss keenly, for he had once extolled the olive as "the richest gift of heaven." As a substitute, he made oil from sesame seeds. He liked the flavor and even purchased his own press so that he could continue to make it at Monticello.

Jefferson's love of vegetables encompassed several other plants as well. He was one of the first Virginians to grow and eat tomatoes, or "tomatas," as he called them. Most Americans thought the tomato was poisonous (and, indeed, it is a member of the deadly nightshade family, though its low toxicity levels pose no risk to humans), and so it was an astonishing event when, in 1806, Jefferson served them to guests at the President's House.[17] Cabbage was another favorite vegetable of Jefferson's; Lemaire records fifty-one purchases in 1806 alone. At Monticello, Jefferson not only raised his own cabbage—eighteen varieties in all—he also bought some from his slaves. Closely related to cabbage is sea kale, which was also grown at Monticello; Jefferson found a variety that was perennial, thus eliminating the expense of purchasing seedlings every year.[18] In 1812 Jefferson became the first gardener in his neighborhood to plant the hot Texas bird pepper, which his cooks used to spice up sauces. And he must have been fond of asparagus, too.

Although he devoted only one square in his garden to the vegetable, he tended it with special care, mulching the plot with tobacco leaves and fertilizing it with manure. His Garden Book includes entries for twenty-two years that record the date on which the first plate of asparagus was brought to his table.[19]

African Dishes on Monticello's Table

The ships that carried kidnapped Africans to America's shores also brought along indigenous crops. Before setting out from Africa's west coast, ship captains purchased local provisions to feed their enslaved passengers confined in the hold. One French slave trader, John Barbot, advised that "a ship that takes in 500 slaves, must provide above 100,000 yams," which works out to two hundred yams per person. Among other common African starches, nuts, vegetables, and fruits that supplied the slave ships were black-eyed peas, peanuts, okra, watermelon, millet, sorghum, and sesame.[1] Eventually, seeds from this African produce made their way into American gardens. At Monticello, okra, black-eyed peas, and peanuts grew in Jefferson's thousand-foot-long garden; his field slaves grew watermelons in their own plots. (Jefferson called peanuts "peendars" or "pindars," from *mpinda*, the Congo word for the legume.)

Every week, each adult slave at Monticello received a ration, which consisted of a peck of cornmeal, a half pound of pork or pickled beef, and four salted fish. On special occasions, such as Christmas, Jefferson would give his slaves a little whiskey. From time to time, if he had an excess of milk or peas or potatoes, he would distribute these items to his slaves, too.[2] It was a monotonous diet, which the slaves supplemented with foods they raised themselves. Every slave cabin at Monticello had its own garden and a run for chickens. Many slaves hunted or fished, and the children collected nuts and berries in the woods. Whatever surplus they produced, the slaves carried to the house. The Monticello household accounts books reveal that the Jefferson women routinely purchased eggs, chickens, cabbages, watermelons, cucumbers, and other produce from their slaves. After a successful fishing, hunting, or trapping expedition, slave men and boys sold what they didn't need to the Jeffersons. With the money from these sales, the slaves purchased extra clothes, tea, coffee, and other small luxuries from shops in Charlottesville.[3]

All the chefs at Monticello were slaves—James Hemings and Peter Hemings, then Edith Fossett, followed by her son Peter Fossett. Although they were trained in the preparation of French cuisine as well as familiar plantation fare, they also served the types of dishes they made for themselves. In Jefferson's Garden Book we find annotations indicating when he dined on watermelon or when a dish of black-eyed peas

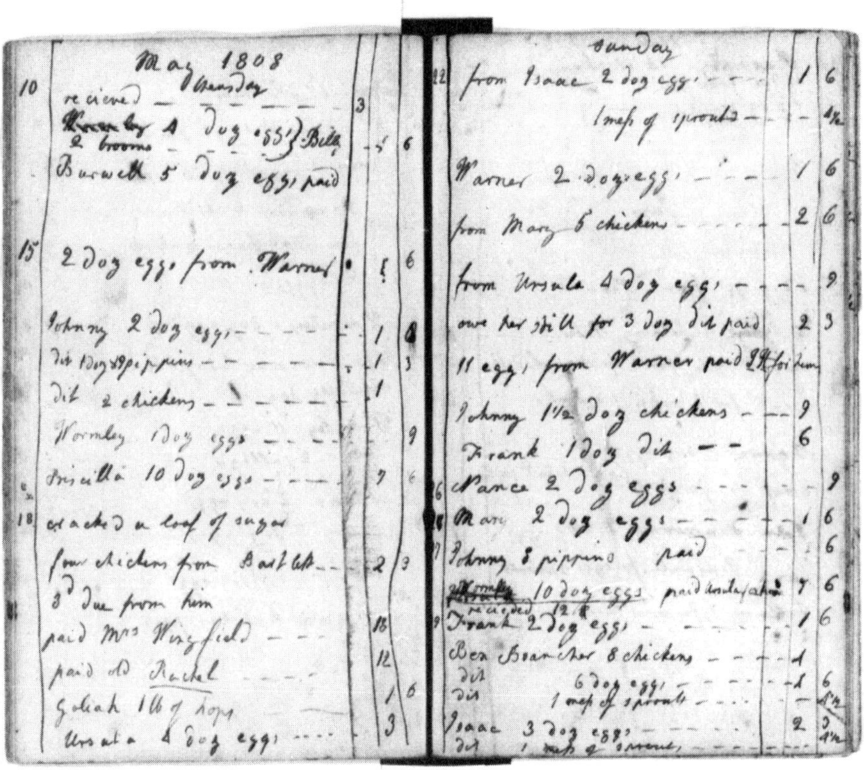

May 1808

```
10  recieved — Tuesday        3
    Wormley 1 dog eggs? Bill    5  6
    Burwell 5 dog eggs paid

15  2 dog eggs from Warner       5  6

    Johnny 2 dog eggs —          1  4
    Dit Dog & pippins —          1  3
    Dit 2 chickens —               1
    Wormley 1 dog eggs —           9
    Priscilla 10 dog eggs —      7  6
18  cracked a loaf of sugar
    four chickens from Bartlet   2  3
    3 due from him
    paid Mrs Wingfield          18
    paid old Rachel             12
    Goliah 1 lb of hops          1  6
    Ursula 4 dog eggs            3
```

```
                  Sunday
22  from Isaac 2 dog eggs           1  6
        1 mess of sprouts              4½
    Warner 2 dog eggs               1  6
    from Mary 5 chickens            2  6
    from Ursula 4 dog eggs             9
    owe her still for 3 dog dit paid 2  3
    11 eggs from Warner paid ...
    Johnny 1½ dog chickens             9
    Frank 1 dog dit                   6
    Nance 2 dog eggs                   9
    Mary 2 dog eggs                 1  6
    Johnny 5 pippins      paid        6
    10 dog eggs  paid Ursula ...    7  6
    recieved 12.6
    Frank 2 dog eggs                1  6
    Ben Bowler 8 chickens          4
    dit       6 dog eggs           1  6
    dit       1 mess of sprouts       4½
    Isaac 3 dog eggs               2  3
    dit   1 mess of sprouts            4½
```

Pages from the Monticello household accounts book, 1808. Jefferson's granddaughter Anne Cary Randolph recorded some of the items purchased from enslaved members of the Monticello estate. (Courtesy Library of Congress, Manuscript Division, Thomas Jefferson Papers) was served at his table.[4] The peas may have been prepared in the classic manner, boiled with greens and slices of salt pork. It is also possible that Jefferson ate that Southern staple transplanted from West Africa: hoppin' john, black-eyed peas cooked with rice.[5]

One of Jefferson's granddaughters, Virginia Randolph, copied as many Monticello recipes as she could find. These include French recipes handed down from either James Hemings, Honoré Julien, or Étienne Lemaire, as well as recipes that came from the slaves, such as gumbo. There are two Monticello recipes for gumbo (its African names are *ngombo* or, perhaps, *kingombo*), a type of stew that originated in Africa.[6] The first calls for equal amounts of okra and tomatoes, peeled and chopped and then sautéed with onions. In another pot, meat is fried in butter. The recipe states that "any kind of meat [may be used], but veal or chicken is best." Once the vegetables are soft and the meat is fried to a golden brown, everything is placed in a soup pot to stew for fifteen minutes. The second recipe calls for the addition of sassafras leaves, which brought another culinary influence to Jefferson's table: enslaved Africans taught the Indian tribes of the Southeast how to make gumbo, and the Indians put their own spin on it by adding sassafras.[7]

There are also recipes for two varieties of okra soup. The simplest one calls for okra, lima beans, tomatoes, and the meat of any available fowl. To thicken the soup, the cook is directed to "put in a lump of butter as big as an egg, rolled in flour." The other, more complicated recipe insists on using only young okra. "If good, they snap," the recipe reads, "if they bend, they are too old." The okra is cooked with corn, lima beans, tomatoes, and a beef shin. All the ingredients simmer together for five hours. The cook knows the soup is done when the meat "is boiled to rags and quits the bone."[8]

Deep-frying chicken is believed to be an African technique that was introduced to America. It has become an American classic, one that is especially associated with the South. At Monticello, fried chicken was served with fried disks of cornmeal mush and a cream gravy.[9]

The gardens at Monticello also grew sesame. Jefferson tells us the seeds were tossed in a salad, added to soup, cooked with greens, or baked in bread.[10] The seeds were also pressed to make sesame oil as a substitute for pricey imported olive oil.

Of course, the chefs at Monticello were not producing all this food alone. It took a small army of household servants to prepare the meals. Young boys such as Israel Gillette brought in coal and firewood, drew water, and carried in frozen blocks from the ice house. They also peeled and chopped vegetables and turned the crank on the ice-cream machine. Men butchered the raw meat, and then the most skilled among them carved it when it was ready to be served. The chef's female assistants tended the soups and stews, the roasting meat, and the simmering vegetables. More complicated preparations, such as sauces and desserts, were left to the chef or were performed under the chef's close supervision.

Of course, there were many more tasks outside the kitchen as well. Women churned cream into butter, brewed beer, and made cider. A Monticello slave named Ursula crafted what Jefferson considered to be the best cider in the neighborhood, reporting that, in cider-making, she "unites trust and skill to do it." Men salted and smoked the meat.[11] Even when sick, the slaves were involved in food preparation. When a slave named Nace fell ill, Jefferson gave instructions that he should be "entirely kept from labour until he recovers," remaining in his cabin where he could shell corn.[12]

A Selection of
Thomas Jefferson's and
James Hemings's Recipes

None of the original cookbooks from Monticello have survived, and only a handful of recipes written by Thomas Jefferson or James Hemings exist. There were many more, transcribed by Jefferson's granddaughter Virginia Randolph Trist (1801–1882). Her original recipes (including those for crème brûlée reproduced on the back cover and the snow eggs mentioned below) were modernized by Marie Kimball in 1938 and appear in the collection titled *Thomas Jefferson's Cook Book*. It is likely that other recipes from Monticello appear in the 1824 cookbook *The Virginia Housewife* by Mary Randolph (1762–1828), Patsy Jefferson's sister-in-law. The following pages present undated recipes recorded by Thomas Jefferson as well as a nineteenth-century transcription of a recipe that Virginia Trist attributed to "James, cook at Monticello." Bon appétit!

les pesches. vous boucher bien vos bouteilles
et le tout est fini.

Peser vos pesches. sur 4. livres de pesches
un livre de sucre et un pinte d'eau de vie.

To preserve haricots verts for winter use.
Take a tight barrel, with one head out, &
set it up an-end. let your snaps be green
but their moisture dried out a little. lay
in a layer of salt & a layer of beans alter-
nately, each about a finger thick, & finish
with a layer of salt. lay the loose head on
them & weight it pretty well down with
stones.
about 2 bushels of beans will serve a
family the winter.

*Ever the farmer, Jefferson sought access to a year-round supply of
fresh produce from his estate. In this recipe for preserving French
green beans, or haricots verts, for winter, he advises: "Let your snaps
be green but their moisture dried out a little." (Courtesy Library of
Congress, Manuscript Division, Thomas Jefferson Papers)*

Several recipes written by Thomas Jefferson are in a mixture of French and English. The macaron recipe contains a helpful hint about baking temperature: "You prove the proper heat of the oven by holding in it a bit of white paper. If it burns, it will burn your macarons, if it just browns the paper[,] it is exact." (Courtesy Library of Congress, Manuscript Division, Thomas Jefferson Papers)

Ice cream.

2 bottles of good cream.
6. yolks of eggs.
½ lb sugar.
mix the yolks & sugar
put the cream on a fire in a casse
-role, first putting in a stick of Vanilla.
when near boiling take it off &
pour it gently into the mixture
of eggs & sugar.
stir it well.
put it on the fire again stirring
it thoroughly with a spoon to
prevent it's sticking to the casse
-role.
when near boiling take it off and
strain it thro' a towel.
put it in the Sabottiere
then set it in ice an hour before
it is to be served. put into the
ice a handful of salt.
put ice all round the Sabotiere
i.e. a layer of ice a layer of salt
for three layers.
put salt on the cover lid of the
Sabotiere & cover the whole with
ice.
leave it still half a quarter of an
hour.
then turn the Sabotiere in the
ice 10 minutes.
open it to loosen with a spatule
the ice from the inner sides of
the Sabotiere.
shut it & replace it in the ice
open it from time to time to de-
-tach the ice from the sides
when well taken (prise) stir it
well with the Spatule.
put it in moulds, justling it
well down on the knee.
then put the mould into the
same bucket of ice.
leave it there to the moment
of serving it.
to withdraw it, immerse the
mould in warm water
turning it well till it
will come out & turn it
into a plate.

Ice cream was a delicacy often served to guests at Monticello. Jefferson's is the earliest known American recipe for the frozen treat. In it, he calls for the use of a sabotiere, a bucket-like freezer for making ices. (Courtesy Library of Congress, Manuscript Division, Thomas Jefferson Papers)

Undated recipes for "biscuit de Savoye" (small cakes), "blanc manger," and "wine jellies." Clearly, Jefferson was a fan of desserts as well as of sweetening meat dishes with sugared jellies. (Courtesy Library of Congress, Manuscript Division, Thomas Jefferson Papers)

Nouilly. à' maccaroni

6 eggs. yolks & whites
2 wine glasses of milk
2 ℔ of flour
a little salt
work them together without water,
  and very well.
roll it then with a roller to a pro-
  -per thickness
cut it into small peices which
  roll again with the hand into
  long slips, & then cut them to
  a proper length.
put them into warm water a quarter
  of an hour.
drain them.
dress them as Maccaroni.
but if they are intended for soups
  they are to be put into the soup
  & not into warm water

Jefferson wrote his recipe for "nouilles à maccaroni," or macaroni noodles, on the reverse of his detailed drawing of a pasta maker. (Recipe transcription and image of press are on pages 116 and 117.) (Courtesy Library of Congress, Manuscript Division, Thomas Jefferson Papers)

Petit's method of making coffee

*On one measure of the coffee ground into meal pour three
measures of boiling water.
boil it, on hot ashes lined with coal till the meal disappears from the top, when it will be precipitated.
pour it three times through a flannel strainer.
it will yield 2⅓ measures of clear coffee.
an ounce of coffee meal makes 1½ cup of clear coffee
in this way.
the flannel must be rinsed out in hot or cold water for every making.*

As recorded by Jefferson, Adrien Petit, his maître d'hôtel in Paris
and Philadelphia, prepared coffee in this manner:

On one measure of the coffee ground into meal pour three
measures of boiling water.
boil on hot ashes lined with coal till the meal disappears from
the top, when it will be precipitated.
pour it three times through a flannel strainer.
it will yield 2 1/3 measures of clear coffee.
an ounce of coffee meal makes 1 1/2 cup of clear coffee in this
way.
the flannel must be rinsed out in hot or cold water for every
making.

2.

Snow Eggs.

Take 10 eggs; separate the yolks from the whites and beat the whites as you do for savory cake, till you can turn the vessel bottom upward without their leaving it; when they are well beaten put in 2 spoonfuls of powdered sugar & a little orange flower water or rose water if you prefer it. Put a pint of milk in a saucepan with 6 oz sugar, and orange flower or rose water; when your milk boils, take the whites, spoonful by spoonful & do them in the boiling milk; when sufficiently poached, take them out & lay them on a sieve, take out a part of the milk, according to the thickness you wish to give the custard, beat

This recipe, attributed to "James [Hemings], cook at Monticello," was recorded by Jefferson's granddaughter Virginia. It contains directions for making "snow eggs," a type of custard, followed by a recipe

up the yolks & stir them in
the remainder; as soon as it
thickens take the mixture
from the fire, strain it through
a sieve; dish up your whites
& pour the custard over them.
A little wine stirred in is a
great improvement.

James, cook at Monticello.

Chocolate cream.

Put on your milk, 1 qt. to 2
squares of chocolate; boil it away
one quarter; take it off; let it
cool; & sweeten it; lay a napkin
in a bowl, put 3 gizzards in the
napkin ~~in a bowl~~ & pass the cream
through it four times, as quick as
possible, one person rubbing the
gizzards with a spoon while another
pours. Put it in cups & let the cups
in cold water halfway up their
sides. Let the water on the fire;

for chocolate cream. (Trist Family Papers, 1818-1916, Accession #5385-f, Special Collections, University of Virginia Library, Charlottesville, Va.)

199

CHRONOLOGY

1743 Thomas Jefferson is born on April 13 at Shadwell Plantation in Albemarle County, Virginia, the son of Peter Jefferson and Jane Randolph Jefferson. Six years earlier his father had acquired the 200-acre plantation in exchange for a large bowl of punch.

1760–62 Thomas Jefferson enrolls in the College of William and Mary in Williamsburg, Virginia.

1762 Jefferson studies law under George Wythe, a distinguished jurist who became Jefferson's mentor and one of his most trusted friends. Wythe also introduces Jefferson to wine, including Madeira and claret, two of the most popular types in 18th-century America.

1764 On his 21st birthday, Jefferson takes control of his inheritance. (His father had died in 1757.)

1765 James Hemings is born to Elizabeth (Betty) Hemings, a slave, and John Wayles, her master.

1768 Jefferson is elected to the House of Burgesses, colonial Virginia's legislature. He also begins clearing the mountaintop at Monticello, leveling it for the plantation house he plans to build there.

1770 Shadwell burns to the ground. Jefferson moves to Monticello and takes up residence in a small outbuilding known as the South Pavilion.

1772 On January 1, Jefferson marries Martha Wayles Skelton, a 22-year-old widow. On September 27, Martha gives birth to a daughter, also named Martha, who is called Patsy.

1773 Death of John Wayles, Martha's father, on May 28. Jefferson inherits 11,000 acres and 135 slaves (including Wayles's concubine, Betty Hemings, and the six children he had with her). Jefferson also becomes responsible for his late father-in-law's debts, which total £4,000.

1774 Jefferson publishes *A Summary View of the Rights of British America*, which lists the injustices George III and his government have inflicted on the American colonies.

1775 Jefferson is elected a delegate to the Continental Congress in Philadelphia.

1776 On July 4, the Continental Congress adopts Jefferson's Declaration of Independence, which declares that "all men are created equal" and asserts "that these united colonies are, and of right ought to be free and independent states."

1777 Jefferson writes the "Virginia Statute on Religious Freedom."

1778 On August 1 Martha Jefferson gives birth to Mary, whom the family calls Polly.

1779–1781 Jefferson serves as governor of Virginia. Toward the end of his term, a British army invades Virginia and sends a detachment to arrest Jefferson at Monticello; he and his family escape as the British are riding up the mountain. For the rest of his life, Jefferson's enemies characterize his escape as cowardice.

1782 On May 8 Martha Jefferson gives birth to Lucy Elizabeth. Martha dies on September 6. Jefferson slips into a period of profound grief and depression.

1784 Congress sends Jefferson to France as a commissioner and minister. He takes along his eldest child, Pasty, and sends his younger daughters, Polly and Lucy, to live with his in-laws. He also takes James Hemings to study French cuisine in Paris. James begins taking cooking lessons from Combeaux, a caterer.

1785 Following the death of Lucy, Jefferson sends for Polly. She arrives in Paris attended by James's sister Sally Hemings, then 14 years old.

1787 In spring, Jefferson tours France and northern Italy, sampling food, collecting wine, and smuggling rice out of Lombardy.

1787 During the summer, James completes his training in the kitchen of the Prince of Condé.

1789 On September 17, James prepares a farewell dinner for four of Jefferson's friends, among them the Marquis de Lafayette.

1789 Jefferson, Patsy and Polly, and James and Sally Hemings, return to the United States in November. Jefferson arrives with 86 crates of European kitchen utensils and equipment and hundreds of bottles of wine, cheeses, and ingredients unavailable in America, such as olive oil and Maille mustard.

1790 Jefferson accepts an appointment as secretary of state in the cabinet of President George Washington. James's intention to begin training his brother Peter in French cuisine is postponed so that the former can serve as Jefferson's chef in New York City.

1790 In July, Jefferson uses James's cuisine to put his political rival, Alexander Hamilton, in a mood to compromise regarding the location of the U.S. capital.

1793 On September 15, Jefferson and James sign a contract in which Jefferson promises to grant James his freedom as soon as he trains Peter Hemings to be a French chef.

1796 Jefferson frees James Hemings on February 5. James goes to Philadelphia, where he finds work as a cook.

1797–1801 Jefferson serves as vice president to John Adams.

1800 Jefferson is elected U.S. president.

1801 At Jefferson's invitation, James returns to Monticello to serve as chef de cuisine during the president's summer vacation. Jefferson returns to Washington, D.C., in September. James goes to Baltimore, where he works as a cook in a tavern. After several days of heavy drinking, James kills himself in October. Jefferson sends a friend to Baltimore to learn the details of the "tragical news."

1803 Without consulting Congress, Jefferson purchases from France the vast Louisiana Territory.

1804 Meriwether Lewis and William Clark, along with 45 men, begin the exploration of the Louisiana Territory.

1809 Jefferson fulfills his term of office and retires to Monticello. He completes his 1,000-foot-long vegetable garden.

1815 Jefferson sells his library of almost 7,000 books to Congress; these will form the nucleus of the Library of Congress.

1825 The University of Virginia opens for classes, with Jefferson serving as the first rector, or president.

1826 Jefferson dies at Monticello on July 4. Several hours later, John Adams dies in his home in Quincy, Massachusetts.

Notes

Prologue

1. Katharine E. Harbury, *Colonial Virginia's Cooking Dynasty* (Columbia: University of South Carolina Press, 2004), 41.

2. Quoted in James E. McWilliams, *A Revolution in Eating: How the Quest for Food Shaped America* (New York: Columbia University Press, 2005), 114–15.

3. Harbury, *Colonial Virginia's Cooking Dynasty*, 47.

4. Ibid.

5. The couple had four other children, all of whom died while young: a daughter named Jane, an unnamed son, and two daughters, both named Lucy. Only Martha and Mary (who later chose the nickname Maria) survived to adulthood.

6. Because accidental fires were so frequent, kitchens were separate buildings in most European and American homes, even as late as the early 20th century.

Chapter 1: Americans in Paris

1. Fawn M. Brodie, *Thomas Jefferson: An Intimate History* (1974; reprint, New York: W. W. Norton, 2010), 210.

2. Henry S. Randall, *The Life of Thomas Jefferson* (New York: Derby &

Jackson, 1858), 1:411–12.

3. *Jefferson's Memorandum Books: Accounts, with Legal Records and Miscellany, 1767–1826*, ed. James A. Bear and Lucia Stanton (Princeton, N.J.: Princeton University Press, 1997), 1:556.

4. *The Writings of Thomas Jefferson* (Washington, D.C.: Thomas Jefferson Memorial Association of the United States, 1904), 1:90.

5. Michael Knox Beran, *Jefferson's Demons: Portrait of a Restless Mind* (New York: Free Press, 2003), 210.

6. *Jefferson's Memorandum Books*, 1:536–37.

7. *The Papers of Thomas Jefferson*, ed. Julian Boyd (Princeton, N.J.: Princeton University Press, 1950–), 7:508.

8. Dumas Malone, *Jefferson and the Rights of Man* (Charlottesville: University of Virginia Press, 1951), 2:4–5.

9. Simon Schama, *Citizens: A Chronicle of the French Revolution* (New York: Alfred A. Knopf, 1989), 76.

10. Howard C. Rice Jr., *Thomas Jefferson's Paris* (Princeton, N.J.: Princeton University Press, 1976), 3.

11. Malone, *Jefferson and the Rights of Man*, 2:5.

12. Stacy Schiff, *A Great Improvisation: Franklin, France, and the Birth of America* (New York: Henry Holt, 2005), 296.

13. *Diary of John Quincy Adams*, ed. David Grayson Allen et al. (Cambridge, Mass.: Belknap Press of Harvard University Press, 1981), 2:147.

14. Thomas Fleming, "Franklin Charms Paris," *American Heritage* 60, no. 1 (spring 2010): 103.

15. Walter Isaacson, *Benjamin Franklin: An American Life* (New York: Simon & Schuster, 2003), 353.

16. Thomas J. Schaeper, *France and America in the Revolutionary Era: The Life of Jacques-Donatien Leray de Chaumont, 1725–1803* (New York and Oxford: Berghahn Books, 1995), 100–101.

17. Isaacson, *Benjamin Franklin*, 428–29.

18. David McCullough, *John Adams* (New York: Simon & Schuster, 2001), 300.

19. Cited in McCullough, *John Adams*, 301.

20. *Diary of John Quincy Adams*, 1:217.

21. Ibid., 218.

22. Ibid., 218–19.

23. Annette Gordon-Reed, *The Hemingses of Monticello: An American Family* (New York: W. W. Norton, 2008), 80.

24. Lucia C. Stanton, *Slavery at Monticello* (Charlottesville, Va.: Thomas Jefferson Foundation, 1993), 13.

25. *Mary Chesnut's Civil War*, ed. C. Vann Woodward (New Haven, Conn.: Yale University Press, 1981), 29.

26. Stanton, *Slavery at Monticello*, 14.

27. Ibid., 13.

28. *Thomas Jefferson's Monticello*, "Thomas Jefferson and Slavery," http://www.monticello.org/site/plantation-and-slavery/thomas-jefferson-and-slavery (accessed April 11, 2012).

29. *Papers of Thomas Jefferson*, 159.

Chapter 2: A Free City

1. *The Papers of Thomas Jefferson*, ed. Julian Boyd (Princeton, N.J.: Princeton University Press, 1950–), 9:254.

2. Annette Gordon-Reed, *The Hemingses of Monticello: An American Family* (New York: W. W. Norton, 2008), 165.

3. *The Works of John Adams, Second President of the United States*, ed., Charles Francis Adams (Boston, Mass.: Little, Brown, 1856), 8:47.

4. *New York Society Library*, "Bringing Home the Exotic: François-Jean Chastellux, Travels in North America (1787)," http://www.nysoclib.org/exhibitions/travel/chastellux_fran-

cois.html (accessed March 7, 2012).

5. Howard C. Rice Jr., *Thomas Jefferson's Paris* (Princeton, N.J.: Princeton University Press, 1976), 64–65.

6. Ibid., 66.

7. Ibid., 52.

8. *Papers of Thomas Jefferson*, 8:472–73.

9. Rice, *Jefferson's Paris*, 51–52.

10. William Howard Adams, *The Paris Years of Thomas Jefferson* (New Haven, Conn.: Yale University Press, 1997), 20.

11. Simon Schama, *Citizens: A Chronicle of the French Revolution* (New York: Alfred A. Knopf, 1989), 26-27.

12. Henry Adams, *History of the United States of America during the Administrations of Thomas Jefferson* (New York: Library of America, 1986), 1:101.

13. Gordon-Reed, *Hemingses of Monticello*, 169.

14. Ibid., 172.

15. Ibid., 172, 175.

16. Ibid., 176.

17. Sue Peabody, *"There Are No Slaves in France": The Political Culture of Race and Slavery in the Ancien Régime* (New York: Oxford University Press, 1996), 4.

18. Gordon-Reed, *Hemingses of Monticello*, 180.

19. David Garrioch, *The Making of Revolutionary Paris* (Berkeley: University of California Press, 2002), 109.

20. Ibid., 110–11.

21. Alistair Horne, *Seven Ages of Paris* (New York: Alfred A. Knopf, 2002), 151.

22. Andrew Hussey, *Paris: The Secret History* (New York: Bloomsbury, 2006), 161.

23. Ibid., 162.

NOTES

24. Horne, *Seven Ages of Paris*, 152–53.

25. Hussey, *Paris*, 163.

26. Ibid., 185–86.

27. C. C. Pearson and J. Edwin Hendricks, *Liquor and Anti-Liquor in Virginia, 1619–1919* (Durham, N.C.: Duke University Press, 1967), 45.

28. Thomas E. Brennan et al., eds., *Public Drinking in the Early Modern World: Voices from the Tavern, 1500–1800* (London: Pickering and Chatto, 2011), 4:191, 188.

29. Daniel Roche, *The People of Paris: An Essay in Popular Culture in the Eighteenth Century* (Berkeley: University of California Press, 1987), 34.

30. Ibid., 53.

31. Olivier Bernier, *Lafayette: Hero of Two Worlds* (New York: E. P. Dutton, 1983), 196.

32. George Green Shackelford, *Thomas Jefferson's Travels in Europe, 1784–1789* (Baltimore, Md.: Johns Hopkins University Press, 1995), 17–18.

33. *Diary of John Quincy Adams*, ed. David Grayson Allen et al. (Cambridge, Mass.: Belknap Press of Harvard University Press, 1981), 1:243–44.

Chapter 3: A Feast for the Palate

1. Quoted in Esther B. Aresty, *The Exquisite Table: A History of French Cuisine* (Indianapolis, Ind.: Bobbs-Merrill, 1980), 42.

2. Ibid., 43.

3. Barbara Ketcham Wheaton, *Savoring the Past: The French Kitchen and Table from 1300 to 1789* (Philadelphia: University of Pennsylvania Press, 1983), 205.

4. Aresty, *Exquisite Table*, 43–44.

5. Wheaton, *Savoring the Past*, 209.

6. Ibid., 224–25.

7. Ibid., 232.

8. Aresty, *Exquisite Table*, 49–50.

9. Ibid., 51–52.

10. Wheaton, *Savoring the Past*, 201–2.

11. Aresty, *Exquisite Table*, 52–53, 55.

12. Ibid., 59–60.

13. Ibid., 60–61.

14. Ibid., 64.

15. Ibid., 65.

16. Wheaton, *Savoring the Past*, 213.

17. Cited in ibid.

18. Cited in ibid., 215.

19. Ibid., 216.

20. Rebecca L. Spang, *The Invention of the Restaurant: Paris and Modern Gastronomic Culture* (Cambridge, Mass.: Harvard University Press, 2000), 1–2.

21. Ibid., 36.

22. Ibid., 7–8.

23. Ibid., 8.

24. Ibid., 8–9.

25. Ibid., 54–57.

26. Ibid., 65, 79–81.

27. Aresty, *Exquisite Table*, 66.

28. John Reader, *Potato: A History of the Propitious Esculent* (New Haven, Conn.: Yale University Press, 2009), 120.

29. *What's Cooking America,* "Potatoes: History of Potatoes," http://whatscookingamerica.net/History/PotatoHistory.htm (accessed March 7, 2012).

30. Reader, *Potato*, 120–22.

31. Frances Phipps, *Colonial Kitchens, Their Furnishings, and Their Gardens* (Portland, Ore.: Hawthorn Books, 1972), 97–98.

32. Louis B. Wright and Marion Tinling, eds., *The Secret Diary of William Byrd of Westover, 1709–1712* (Petersburg, Va.: Dietz Press, 1941), 316.

Chapter 4: The Wine Collector and Rice Smuggler

1. George Green Shackelford, *Thomas Jefferson's Travels in Europe, 1784–1789* (Baltimore, Md.: Johns Hopkins University Press, 1995), 75.

2. *The Papers of Thomas Jefferson*, ed. Julian Boyd (Princeton, N.J.: Princeton University Press, 1950–), 11:215.

3. Ibid., 10:612.

4. Ibid., 11:477.

5. James M. Gabler, *Passions: The Wines and Travels of Thomas Jefferson* (Emeryville, Calif.: Bacchus Press, 1995), 59.

6. Ibid.

7. Jancis Robinson, ed., *The Oxford Companion to Wine*, 3rd ed. (New York: Oxford University Press, 2006), 150–53.

8. *Papers of Thomas Jefferson*, 11:415.

9. Ibid., 13:31.

10. Ibid., 11:285.

11. Ibid., 13:313.

12. Eric Pfanner, "In Burgundy, It's All About Terroir," *New York Times*, September 16, 2011.

13. Gabler, *Passions*, 62.

14. Ibid., 63.

15. Ibid., 64.

16. Ibid., 65.

17. Shackelford, *Thomas Jefferson's Travels in Europe*, 79.

18. *Papers of Thomas Jefferson*, 11:418–20.

19. Ibid., 11:420.

20. Ibid., 11:421.

21. Ibid., 11:226.

22. Ibid., 11:423.

23. Gabler, *Passions*, 73.

24. Ibid., 77.

25. Ibid., 86.

26. *Papers of Thomas Jefferson*, 10:280.

27. *Papers of Thomas Jefferson*, 18:247.

28. Gabler, *Passions*, 87.

29. *Papers of Thomas Jefferson*, 11:283.

30. *The Writings of Thomas Jefferson* (Washington, D.C.: Thomas Jefferson Memorial Association of the United States, 1904), 19:33.

31. *Papers of Thomas Jefferson*, 18:432.

32. Shackelford, *Thomas Jefferson's Travels in Europe*, 90.

33. *Thomas Jefferson: Writings*, ed. Merrill D. Peterson (New York: Library of America, 1984), 792.

34. Lucia C. Stanton, "Mediterranean Journey, 1787," *Monticello Keepsake*, April 12, 1987.

Chapter 5: Brother and Sister, Reunited

1. *The Papers of Thomas Jefferson*, ed. Julian Boyd (Princeton, N.J.: Princeton University Press, 1950–), 7:616.

2. Ibid., 7:538–39.

3. Ibid., 7:441.

4. Abigail Adams Smith, *Journal and Correspondence* (New York: Wiley & Putnam, 1841), 45.

5. Fawn M. Brodie, *Thomas Jefferson: An Intimate History* (Bantam Books, 1979), 191.

6. Lucia C. Stanton, *Free Some Day: The African-American Families of Monticello* (Charlottesville, Va.: Thomas Jefferson Foundation, 2000), 108.

7. Thomas Fleming, *Intimate Lives of the Founding Fathers* (New York: HarperCollins, 2010), 303.

8. *Papers of Thomas Jefferson*, 11:573.

9. Ibid., 11:575.

10. Brodie, *Thomas Jefferson*, 277.

11. *Papers of Thomas Jefferson*, 11:551.

12. Annette Gordon-Reed, *The Hemingses of Monticello: An American Family* (1974; reprint, New York: W. W. Norton, 2010), 229.

13. David McCullough, *John Adams* (New York: Simon & Schuster, 2001), 373.

14. Ibid.

15. Gordon-Reed, *Hemingses of Monticello*, 229–30.

16. Cited in Virginia Scharff, *The Women Jefferson Loved* (New York: HarperCollins, 2010), 182.

17. Elizabeth A. Fenn, *Pox Americana: The Great Smallpox Epidemic of 1775–82* (New York: Hill and Wang, 2001), 273.

18. *Thomas Jefferson's Monticello*, "Inoculation," http://www.monticello .org/site/research-and-collections/inoculation (accessed April 12, 2012).

19. Howard C. Rice Jr., *Thomas Jefferson's Paris* (Princeton, N.J.: Princeton University Press, 1976), 104–5.

20. Simon Schama, *Citizens: A Chronicle of the French Revolution* (New York: Alfred A. Knopf, 1989), 771–74.

21. Gordon-Reed, *Hemingses of Monticello*, 251.

22. Ibid., 166.

23. Ibid., 167.

24. Priscilla Parkhurst Ferguson, *Accounting for Taste: The Triumph of*

French Cuisine (Chicago: University of Chicago Press, 2004), 135.

25. Ibid., 139.

26. Jessica B. Harris, *High on the Hog: A Culinary Journey from Africa to America* (New York: Bloomsbury, 2011), 80.

27. Gordon-Reed, *Hemingses of Monticello*, 209–10.

28. Ibid., 227.

29. *Thomas Jefferson's Monticello*, "Maria Cosway, Engraving," http://www.monticello.org/site/research-and-collections/maria-cosway-engraving (accessed April 12, 2012).

30. Merrill D. Peterson, ed., *Visitors to Monticello* (Charlottesville: University of Virginia Press, 1989), 28.

31. Damon Lee Fowler, ed., *Dining at Monticello: In Good Taste and Abundance* (Charlottesville, Va.: Thomas Jefferson Foundation, 2005), 102.

Chapter 6: Boiling Point

1. Fawn M. Brodie, *Thomas Jefferson: An Intimate History* (1974; reprint, New York: W. W. Norton, 2010), 305.

2. Samuel Eliot Morison, *The Oxford History of the American People* (New York: Oxford University Press, 1972), 361.

3. *The Papers of Thomas Jefferson, Retirement Series*, ed. J. Jefferson Looney (Princeton, N.J.: Princeton University Press, 2005–), 7:248.

4. Brodie, *Thomas Jefferson*, 310.

5. *The Papers of Thomas Jefferson*, ed. Julian Boyd (Princeton, N.J.: Princeton University Press, 1950–), 14:426.

6. Franklin L. Ford, *Europe, 1780–1830*, 2nd ed. (London: Longman, 1989), 102.

7. Simon Schama, *Citizens: A Chronicle of the French Revolution* (New York: Alfred A. Knopf, 1989), 296–97.

8. Ibid., 399.

9. Ibid., 400.

10 Ibid., 403.

11. Ibid., 404–5.

12. Ibid., 420.

13. Boyd, *Papers of Thomas Jefferson*, 8:404–6.

14. *Thomas Jefferson: Writings*, ed. Merrill D. Peterson (New York: Library of America, 1984), 78.

15. Antonia Fraser, *Marie Antoinette: The Journey* (New York: Nan A. Talese-Doubleday, 2001), 279–80.

16. William Howard Adams, *The Paris Years of Thomas Jefferson* (New Haven, Conn.: Yale University Press, 1997), 254–55.

17. Boyd, *Papers of Thomas Jefferson*, 11: 482.

18. Adams, *Paris Years of Thomas Jefferson*, 273–75.

19. Boyd, *Papers of Thomas Jefferson*, 15:10.

20. Adams, *Paris Years of Thomas Jefferson*, 286–87.

21. Boyd, *Papers of Thomas Jefferson*, 15:326.

22. Ibid., 307.

23. Ibid., 426.

24. Brodie, *Thomas Jefferson*, 313.

25. Boyd, *Papers of Thomas Jefferson*, 15:375.

26. Brodie, *Thomas Jefferson*, 314.

27. Adams, *Paris Years of Thomas Jefferson*, 5.

28. Gouverneur Morris, *A Diary of the French Revolution*, ed. Beatrix Cary Davenport (Boston: Houghton Mifflin, 1939), 1:259.

29. Adams, *Paris Years of Thomas Jefferson*, 10.

30. Ibid., 10–11, 113.

31. Morris, *Diary of the French Revolution*, 221.

32. Adams, *Paris Years of Thomas Jefferson*, 19.

33. Brodie, *Thomas Jefferson*, 314.

34. Anna Stockwell, "Cooking Art History: A Jeffersonian Feast,"

    Saveur, February 23, 2011, http://www.saveur.com/article/
    Kitchen/Cooking-Art-History-A-Jeffersonian-Feast (accessed
    April 19, 2012).

35. Brodie, *Thomas Jefferson*, 314.

36. Ibid., 315.

37. Adams, *Paris Years of Thomas Jefferson*, 23.

38. Boyd, *Papers of Thomas Jefferson*, 15:512.

Chapter 7: The Art of the Meal

1. Fawn M. Brodie, *Thomas Jefferson: An Intimate History* (1974; reprint,
    New York: W. W. Norton, 2010), 31.

2. Charles A. Cerami, *Dinner at Mr. Jefferson's: Three Men, Five Great
    Wines, and the Evening That Changed America* (Hoboken: N.J.:
    Wiley, 2008), 1.

3. Joseph. J. Ellis, *Founding Brothers: The Revolutionary Generation* (New
    York: Alfred A. Knopf, 2000), 140.

4. Cerami, *Dinner at Mr. Jefferson's*, 119.

5. Noble E. Cunningham Jr., *Jefferson vs. Hamilton: Confrontations That
    Shaped a Nation* (New York: Macmillan, 2000), 37.

6. Dumas Malone, *Jefferson and the Rights of Man* (Charlottesville: Uni-
    versity of Virginia Press, 1951), 2:301.

7. Cerami, *Dinner at Mr. Jefferson's*, 129–33.

8. Cunningham, *Jefferson vs. Hamilton*, 37.

9. Ellis, *Founding Brothers*, 153–54.

10. *The Papers of Thomas Jefferson*, ed. John Catanzariti (Princeton, N.J.:
    Princeton University Press, 1950–), 24:354–5.

11. Brodie, *Thomas Jefferson*, 359.

12. *Thomas Jefferson's Farm Book*, ed. Edwin Morris Betts (Chapel Hill,
    NC: University of North Carolina Press, 1955 (1944; reprint:
    Charlottesville, Va.: Thomas Jefferson Memorial Foundation,

1999), 15–16

13. Lucia C. Stanton, *Free Some Day: The African-American Families of Monticello* (Charlottesville, Va.: Thomas Jefferson Foundation, 2000), 17.

14. Damon Lee Fowler, ed., *Dining at Monticello: In Good Taste and Abundance* (Charlottesville, Va.: Thomas Jefferson Foundation, 2005), 23–25.

15. [Isaac Jefferson], *Memoirs of a Monticello Slave as Dictated to Charles Campbell in the 1840's by Isaac, one of Thomas Jefferson's Slaves*, ed. Rayford W. Logan (Charlottesville: University of Virginia Press, 1951), 29.

16. Fowler, *Dining at Monticello*, 42.

17. [Jefferson], *Memoirs of a Monticello Slave*, 29.

18. Fowler, *Dining at Monticello*, 73.

19. *Papers of Thomas Jefferson*, 28:605.

20. Ibid., 28:611.

21. Stanton, *Free Some Day*, 127.

22. Lester J. Cappon, ed., *The Adams–Jefferson Letters: The Complete Correspondence Between Thomas Jefferson and Abigail and John Adams* (Chapel Hill: University of North Carolina Press, 1959), 249.

23. James Sterling Young, *The Washington Community, 1800–1828* (New York: Harcourt, Brace & World, 1966), 167, 169–70.

24. William Plumer Jr., ed., *Life of William Plumer* (Boston, Mass.: Phillips, Sampson, 1857), 245–46.

25. William Parker Cutler et al., eds., *Life, Journals and Correspondence of Rev. Manasseh Cutler, LL.D.* (Cincinnati, Ohio: Robert Clarke, 1888), 2:71–72.

26. Lucia C. Stanton, "'A Well-Ordered Household': Domestic Servants in Jefferson's White House," *White House History* 17 (2006), n.p.

27. *The Papers of Thomas Jefferson*, ed. Barbara B. Oberg (Princeton, N.J.:

Princeton University Press, 2009), 35:89–90.

28. Margaret Bayard Smith, *Forty Years of Washington Society* (New York: Charles Scribner's Sons, 1906), 391–92.

29. Stanton, "A Well-Ordered Household," 9–10.

30. Jean Hanvey Hazelton, "Thomas Jefferson Gourmel'," *American Heritage* 15, no. 6 (October 1964): http://www.american heritage.com/content/thomas-jefferson-gourmel'.

31. Fowler, *Dining at Monticello*, 3.

32. Stanton, *Free Some Day*, 128–29.

33. Fowler, *Dining at Monticello*, 8.

Appendix
The Wine Connoisseur

1. *Thomas Jefferson's Monticello*, "Wine is a necessary of life ... (Quotation)," http://www.monticello.org/site/jefferson/wine-necessary-life-quotation (accessed April 25, 2012).

2. James M. Gabler, "Thomas Jefferson's Love Affair with Wine," *Forbes*, February 21, 2006, http://www.forbes.com/2006/02/21/cx_0221wine4.html (accessed April 25, 2012).

3. *Thomas Jefferson's Monticello*, "Philip Mazzei," http://www.monticello.org/site/research-and-collections/philip-mazzei (accessed April 25, 2012).

4. Richard Cecil Garlick Jr., *Philip Mazzei, Friend of Jefferson: His Life and Letters* (Baltimore, Md.: Johns Hopkins University Press, 1933), 43.

5. *Thomas Jefferson's Monticello*, "Philip Mazzei."

6. Jancis Robinson, ed., *The Oxford Companion to Wine*, 3rd ed. (New York: Oxford University Press, 2006), 416–9.

7. John Hailman, *Thomas Jefferson on Wine* (Jackson: University Press of

Mississippi, 2006), 3–4.

8. Jack McLaughlin, *Jefferson and Monticello: The Biography of a Builder* (New York: Henry Holt, 1988), 234–5.

9. Hailman, *Jefferson on Wine*, 4.

10. Ibid., 17.

11. *Thomas Jefferson's Monticello*, "The Vineyards," http://www.monticello .org/site/house-and-gardens/vineyards (accessed April 25, 2012).

12. *Thomas Jefferson's Monticello*, "Wine," http://www.monticello.org/ site/research-and-collections/wine (accessed April 25, 2012).

Vegetables: Thomas Jefferson's "Principal Diet"

1. *The Writings of Thomas Jefferson* (Washington, D.C.: Thomas Jefferson Memorial Association of the United States, 1904), 15:187.

2. Henry S. Randall, *The Life of Thomas Jefferson* (New York: Derby & Jackson, 1858), 3:675.

3. Charles M. Wiltse, et al., "Notes of Mr. Jefferson's Conversation 1824 at Monticello," *Papers of Daniel Webster: Correspondence* (Hanover, N.H.: University Press of New England, 1974), 1:371.

4. Thomas Jefferson, *Jefferson's Memorandum Books: Accounts, with Legal Records and Miscellany, 1767–1826*, eds. James A. Bear and Lucia Stanton (Princeton, N.J.: Princeton University Press, 1997), 1:73.

5. Thomas Jefferson's Monticello, "Interesting Facts & Stats from 'A Rich Spot of Earth,'" http://www.monticello.org/site/house-and-gardens/richspotofearthfacts (accessed April 25, 2012).

6. *Thomas Jefferson's Garden Book, 1766–1824: With Relevant Extracts from His Other Writings*, ed. Edwin Morris Betts (1944; reprint: Charlottesville, Va.: Thomas Jefferson Memorial Foundation, 1999), xvi.

7. *Thomas Jefferson's Monticello*, "Jefferson: the Scientist and Gardener,"

http://www.monticello.org/site/house-and-gardens/jefferson-scientist-and-gardener (accessed April 25, 2012).

8. *Thomas Jefferson's Monticello*, "Garden Pavilion," http://www.monticello.org/site/house-and-gardens/garden-pavilion (accessed April 25, 2012).

9. *Jefferson's Garden Book*, 355.

10. Lucia C. Stanton, *Free Some Day: The African-American Families of Monticello* (Charlottesville, Va.: Thomas Jefferson Foundation, 2000), 134.

11. *Thomas Jefferson's Monticello*, "19th-Century Vegetables and Cultivation Techniques," http://www.monticello.org/site/house-and-gardens/19th-century-vegetables-and-cultivation-techniques (accessed April 26, 2012).

12. Peter J. Hatch, "Thomas Jefferson's Favorite Vegetables," in *Dining at Monticello: In Good Taste and Abundance*, ed. Damon Lee Fowler (Charlottesville, Va.: Thomas Jefferson Foundation, 2005), 55.

13. Ibid., 56.

14. *Thomas Jefferson's Monticello*, "Bernard McMahon," http://www.monticello.org/site/house-and-gardens/bernard-mcmahon (accessed April 26, 2012).

15. *Thomas Jefferson's Monticello*, "Fun Fact," http://www.monticello.org/site/jefferson/fun-fact-1 (accessed April 26, 2012).

16. Mary Randolph, *The Virginia Housewife: or, Methodical Cook* (Baltimore, Md.: Plaskitt, Fite, 1838), 96.

17. Hatch, "Jefferson's Favorite Vegetables," 57.

18. Ibid., 61.

19. Ibid.

African Dishes on Monticello's Table

1. Joseph E. Holloway, "African Crops and Slave Cuisines," *The Slave Rebellion Web Site*, http://slaverebellion.org/index.php?page=crops-slave-cuisines (accessed April 26, 2012).

2. Dianne Swann-Wright, "African Americans and Monticello's Food Culture," in *Dining at Monticello: In Good Taste and Abundance*, ed. Damon Lee Fowler (Charlottesville, Va.: Thomas Jefferson Foundation, 2005), 43.

3. Lucia C. Stanton, *Slavery at Monticello* (Charlottesville, Va.: Thomas Jefferson Foundation, 1993), 38.

4. Marie Kimball, *Thomas Jefferson's Cook Book* (1938; reprint, Richmond, Va.: Garrett and Massie, 2004), 9.

5. Holloway, "African Crops and Slave Cuisines."

6. Karen Hess, *The Carolina Rice Kitchen: The African Connection* (Columbia: University of South Carolina Press, 1992), 49.

7. Kimball, *Jefferson's Cook Book*, 38–39.

8. Ibid., 40.

9. Ibid., 67.

10. Holloway, "African Crops and Slave Cuisines."

11. Swann-Wright, "African Americans and Monticello's Food Culture," 41.

12. Stanton, *Slavery at Monticello*, 25.

Select Bibliography

Adams, Henry. *History of the United States of America during the Administrations of Thomas Jefferson.* 2 vols. New York: Library of America, 1986.

Adams, John. *The Works of John Adams, Second President of the United States.* Ed. Charles Francis Adams. Boston, Mass.: Little, Brown, 1851.

Adams, John Quincy. *Diary of John Quincy Adams.* 2 vols. Ed. David Grayson Allen. Cambridge, Mass.: Belknap Press of Harvard University Press, 1981.

Adams, William Howard. *The Paris Years of Thomas Jefferson.* New Haven, Conn.: Yale University Press, 1997.

Aresty, Esther B. *The Exquisite Table: A History of French Cuisine.* Indianapolis, Ind.: Bobbs-Merrill, 1980.

Beran, Michael Knox. *Jefferson's Demons: Portrait of a Restless Mind.* New York: Free Press, 2003.

Bernier, Olivier. *Lafayette: Hero of Two Worlds.* New York: E. P. Dutton, 1983.

Betts, Edwin Morris, ed. *Thomas Jefferson's Farm Book.* Chapel Hill: University of North Carolina Press, 1955.

————. *Thomas Jefferson's Garden Book, 1766–1824: With Relevant Extracts from His Other Writings.* 1944; reprint: Charlottesville, Va.: Thomas Jefferson Memorial Foundation, 1999.

Brennan, Thomas E., et al., eds. *Public Drinking in the Early Modern World:*

Voices from the Tavern, 1500–1800. London: Pickering & Chatto, 2011.

Brodie, Fawn M. *Thomas Jefferson: An Intimate History*. 1974; reprint, New York: W. W. Norton, 2010.

Cappon, Lester J., ed. *The Adams–Jefferson Letters: The Complete Correspondence Between Thomas Jefferson and Abigail and John Adams*. Chapel Hill: University of North Carolina Press, 1988.

Cerami, Charles A. *Dinner at Mr. Jefferson's: Three Men, Five Great Wines, and the Evening That Changed America*. Hoboken, N.J.: Wiley, 2008.

Chelminski, Rudolph. *The French at Table*. New York: William Morrow, 1985.

Chesnut, Mary. *Mary Chesnut's Civil War*. Ed. C. Vann Woodward. New Haven, Conn.: Yale University Press, 1981.

Cunningham, Noble E., Jr. *Jefferson vs. Hamilton: Confrontations That Shaped a Nation*. New York: Macmillan, 2000.

Cutler, William P., et al., eds. *Life, Journals, and Correspondence of Rev. Manasseh Cutler, LL.D.* Cincinnati, Ohio: Robert Clarke, 1888.

Ellis, Joseph J. *Founding Brothers: The Revolutionary Generation*. New York: Alfred A. Knopf, 2000.

Fenn, Elizabeth A. *Pox Americana: The Great Smallpox Epidemic of 1775–82*. New York: Hill and Wang, 2001.

Ferguson, Priscilla Parkhurst. *Accounting for Taste: The Triumph of French Cuisine*. Chicago: University of Chicago Press, 2004.

Fleming, Thomas. "Franklin Charms Paris." *American Heritage* 60, no. 1 (spring 2010). http://www.americanheritage.com/content/franklin-charms-paris (accessed March 7, 2012).

———. *Intimate Lives of the Founding Fathers*. New York: Harper Collins, 2010.

Ford, Franklin L. *Europe, 1780–1830*. London: Longman, 2002.

Fowler, Damon Lee, ed. *Dining at Monticello: In Good Taste and Abundance*.

Charlottesville, Va.: Thomas Jefferson Foundation, 2005.

Fraser, Antonia. *Marie Antoinette: The Journey*. New York: Nan A. Talese/Doubleday, 2001.

Gabler, James M. *Passions: The Wines and Travels of Thomas Jefferson*. Baltimore, Md.: Bacchus Press, 1995.

———. "Thomas Jefferson's Love Affair with Wine." *Forbes*, February 21, 2006, http://www.forbes.com/2006/02/21/cx_0221wine4.html (accessed April 25, 2012).

Garrioch, David. *The Making of Revolutionary Paris*. Berkeley and Los Angeles: University of California Press, 2002.

Gordon-Reed, Annette. *The Hemingses of Monticello: An American Family*. New York: W. W. Norton, 2008.

Hailman, John. *Thomas Jefferson on Wine*. Jackson: University Press of Mississippi, 2006.

Harbury, Katharine E. *Colonial Virginia's Cooking Dynasty*. Columbia: University of South Carolina Press, 2004.

Harris, Jessica B. *High on the Hog: A Culinary Journey from Africa to America*. New York: Bloomsbury, 2011.

Hazelton, Jean Hanvey. "Thomas Jefferson Gourmel'." *American Heritage* 15, no. 6 (October 1964). http://www.americanheritage.com/content/thomas-jefferson-gourmel' (accessed March 7, 2012).

Horne, Alistair. *Seven Ages of Paris*. New York: Alfred A. Knopf, 2002.

Hussey, Andrew. *Paris: The Secret History*. New York: Bloomsbury, 2006.

Isaacson, Walter. *Benjamin Franklin: An American Life*. New York: Simon & Schuster, 2003.

[Jefferson, Isaac]. *Memoirs of a Monticello Slave as Dictated to Charles Campbell in the 1840's by Isaac, one of Thomas Jefferson's Slaves*. Ed. Rayford W. Logan. Charlottesville: University of Virginia Press, 1951.

Jefferson, Thomas. *Jefferson's Memorandum Books: Accounts, with Legal Records and Miscellany, 1767–1826*. Eds. James A. Bear and Lucia Stanton. Princeton, N.J.: Princeton University Press, 1997.

———. *The Papers of Thomas Jefferson*. Princeton, N.J.: Princeton University Press, 1950–.

———. *The Papers of Thomas Jefferson, Retirement Series*. Ed. J. Jefferson Looney. Princeton, N.J.: Princeton University Press, 2005–.

———. *Thomas Jefferson: Writings*. Ed. Merrill D. Peterson. New York: Library of America, 1984.

———. *The Writings of Thomas Jefferson*. Vol. 19. Washington, D.C.: Thomas Jefferson Memorial Association of the United States, 1904.

Kimball, Marie. *Thomas Jefferson's Cook Book*. 1938; reprint: Richmond, Va.: Garrett and Massie, 2004.

Lemay, J. A. Leo. *The Life of Benjamin Franklin, Volume 2: Printer and Publisher, 1730–1747*. Philadelphia: University of Pennsylvania Press, 2006.

Malone, Dumas. *Jefferson and the Rights of Man*. Vol. 2. Charlottesville: University of Virginia Press, 1951.

Manceron, Claude. *Their Gracious Pleasure, 1782–1785*. Trans. Nancy Amphoux. New York: Alfred A. Knopf, 1980.

Mann, Charles C. *1493: Uncovering the New World Columbus Created*. New York: Alfred A. Knopf, 2011.

McCullough, David. *John Adams*. New York: Simon & Schuster, 2001.

McLaughlin, Jack. *Jefferson and Monticello: The Biography of a Builder*. New York: Henry Holt, 1988.

McWilliams, James E. *A Revolution in Eating: How the Quest for Food Shaped America*. New York: Columbia University Press, 2005.

Morison, Samuel Eliot. *The Oxford History of the American People*. New York: Oxford University Press, 1972.

Morris, Gouverneur. *A Diary of the French Revolution*. Ed. Beatrix Cary Davenport. 2 vols. Boston: Houghton Mifflin, 1939.

New York Society Library. "Bringing Home the Exotic: François-Jean

Chastellux, Travels in North America (1787)."
http://www.nysoclib.org/exhibitions/travel/chastellux_
francois.html (accessed March 7, 2012).

O'Brien, Conor Cruise. *The Long Affair: Thomas Jefferson and the French
Revolution, 1785–1800.* Chicago: University of Chicago Press,
1996.

Peabody, Sue. *"There Are No Slaves in France": The Political Culture of
Race and Slavery in the Ancien Régime.* New York: Oxford University Press, 1996.

Pearson, C. C., and J. Edwin Hendricks. *Liquor and Anti-Liquor in Virginia,
1619–1919.* Durham, N.C.: Duke University Press, 1967.

Peterson, Merrill D., ed. *Visitors to Monticello.* Charlottesville: University
of Virginia Press, 1989.

Pfanner, Eric. "In Burgundy, It's All About Terroir." *New York Times,*
September 16, 2011.

Phipps, Frances. *Colonial Kitchens, Their Furnishings, and Their Gardens.*
Portland, Ore.: Hawthorn Books, 1972.

Plumer, William, Jr., ed. *Life of William Plumer.* Boston, Mass.: Phillips,
Sampson, 1857.

Randall, Henry S. *The Life of Thomas Jefferson.* 3 vols. New York: Derby
& Jackson, 1858.

Randolph, Mary. *The Virginia Housewife: or, Methodical Cook.* Baltimore,
Md.: Plaskitt, Fite, 1838.

Reader, John. *Potato: A History of the Propitious Esculent.* New Haven,
Conn.: Yale University Press, 2009.

Rein, Lisa. "Mystery of Va.'s First Slaves Is Unlocked 400 Years Later."
Washington Post, September 3, 2006.

Rice, Howard C., Jr. *Thomas Jefferson's Paris.* Princeton, N.J.: Princeton
University Press, 1976.

Robinson, Jancis, ed. *The Oxford Companion to Wine.* 3rd ed. New York:

Oxford University Press, 2006.

Roche, Daniel. *The People of Paris: An Essay in Popular Culture in the 18th Century.* Berkeley and Los Angeles: University of California Press, 1987.

Schaeper, Thomas J. *France and America in the Revolutionary Era: The Life of Jacques-Donatien Leray de Chaumont, 1725–1803.* Brooklyn, N.Y., and Oxford, Eng.: Berghahn Books, 1995.

Schama, Simon. *Citizens: A Chronicle of the French Revolution.* New York: Alfred A. Knopf, 1989.

Scharff, Virginia. *The Women Jefferson Loved.* New York: HarperCollins, 2010.

Schiff, Stacy. *A Great Improvisation: Franklin, France, and the Birth of America.* New York: Henry Holt, 2005.

Shackelford, George Green. *Thomas Jefferson's Travels in Europe, 1784–1789.* Baltimore, Md.: Johns Hopkins University Press, 1995.

Slavery in the North. "Northern Emancipation." http://www.slavenorth.com/emancipation.html (accessed March 7, 2012).

Smith, Abigail Adams. *Journal and Correspondence of Miss Adams.* New York: Wiley and Putnam, 1841.

Smith, Adam. *An Inquiry into the Nature and Causes of the Wealth of Nations.* London: Methuen, 1904.

Smith, Margaret Bayard. *Forty Years of Washington Society.* New York: Charles Scribner's Sons, 1906.

Spang, Rebecca L. *The Invention of the Restaurant: Paris and Modern Gastronomic Culture.* Cambridge, Mass.: Harvard University Press, 2000.

Stanton, Lucia C. "'A Well-Ordered Household': Domestic Servants in Jefferson's White House." Washington, D.C.: *White House History* 17, 2006.

———. *Free Some Day: The African-American Families of Monticello.*

Charlottesville, Va.: Thomas Jefferson Foundation, 2000.

———. "Mediterranean Journey, 1787." *Monticello Keepsake*, April 12, 1987.

———. *Slavery at Monticello*. Charlottesville, Va.: Thomas Jefferson Foundation, 1993.

Stockwell, Anna. "Cooking Art History: A Jeffersonian Feast." *Saveur*, February 23, 2011. http://www.saveur.com/article/Kitchen/Cooking-Art-History-A-Jeffersonian-Feast (accessed April 19, 2012).

Tannahil, Reay. *Food in History*. New York: Stein and Day, 1973.

Thomas Jefferson's Monticello. http://www.monticello.org (accessed April 25, 2012).

Visser, Margaret. *Much Depends on Dinner: The Extraordinary History and Mythology, Allure and Obsessions, Perils and Taboos of an Ordinary Meal*. Toronto: McClelland and Stewart, 1987.

What's Cooking America. "Potatoes: History of Potatoes." http://whatscookingamerica.net/History/PotatoHistory.htm (accessed March 7, 2012).

Wheaton, Barbara Ketcham. *Savoring the Past: The French Kitchen and Table from 1300 to 1789*. Philadelphia: University of Pennsylvania Press, 1983.

Wiltse, Charles M., et al. "Notes of Mr. Jefferson's Conversation 1824 at Monticello." *Papers of Daniel Webster: Correspondence*. Vol. 1. Hanover, N.H.: University Press of New England, 1974.

Wright, Louis B., and Marion Tinling, eds. *The Secret Diary of William Byrd of Westover, 1709–1712*. Petersburg, Va.: Dietz Press, 1941.

Young, James Sterling. *The Washington Community, 1800–1828*. New York: Harcourt, Brace & World, 1966.

Zanger, Mark H. *The American History Cookbook*. Santa Barbara, Calif.: Greenwood Press, 2003.

Index

accidents, 75, 78
Adams, Abigail, 31–33, 42, 60, 103–5
Adams, John
    Auteuil, 31–33, 55, 60
    commissioner to France, 18, 25
    death, 162, 204
    family, 31–33
    on Franklin, 27–29
    hard cider consumption, 52
    and Jefferson, 32–33, 103, 154
Adams, John Quincy, 17–18, 31, 56–57, 173
Adams, Nabby, 31, 33, 101
African foods, 3, 185–90
alcoholic beverages, 52, 53, 68, 170, 190. *See also* wine
ambassadors, 26, 32
American Revolution, 201–2
    debts from, 143–44
    French involvement, 6–7, 21, 26–27, 29, 38
    Italian support, 171
    See also Declaration of Independence
Antoinette, Marie, 51, 56, 74, 129–30
archaeology, 4, 180
architecture
    Palladian, 174
    Paris, 21, 22, 50–51, 55
    Roman, 87–89, 91
art and artists, 21, 78, 87, 136–37, 163
asparagus, 184

Bachet, Jean-Joseph, 86
Bacon, Nathaniel, 4
Bailey, Robert, 180
baked beans, 5
du Barry, Jeanne, 65
Bastille, 54, 125–28, 131–32
beans, baked, 5
de Beauharnais, Joséphine, 40
Beaujolais (province), 60, 86–87
Beaujolais (wine), 67
Beaune, 85
de Beauvoir, François-Jean, 38–39
beggars, 20
Bergasse, Henri, 92–93
Bonaparte, Napoleon, 40
Bordeaux (province), 96
Bordeaux (wine), 38, 171, 174
Bradford, William, 5
bread, 60, 64, 135–36, 156
bridges, 22, 55

Burgundy (province), 81, 83–85
Burgundy (wine), 42, 60

cabbage, 183
cafés, 51–52
de Calonne, Charles, 122–23
canals, 96
carriages, 20, 50, 77–78, 79
caterers, 69, 164. *See also* Combeaux
Cathedral of Notre-Dame, 40, 55–57, 132
Catholics, 109, 119–21, 122–23, 172
Chambertin, 84, 172
Champagne (province), 80–82
Champagne (wine), 80, 82, 113, 165, 172–73
Champs-Elysées, 22, 23, 108
Chantilly chateau, 110–11
Charles, Prince de Soubise, 14
de Chastellux, Marquis, 38–39
chefs/cooks
    Julia Child, 16, 165–66
    in France, 2, 61, 65–67, 111–12
    at Monticello, 151, 155–56, 159, 186
    in Virginia, 3
    in Washington, 163–64
    See also Hemings, James
china, 9, 64, 74
churches, 21, 40, 55–57, 87, 132
clothing and dress
    Marie Antoinette, 130
    Benjamin Franklin, 26
    Thomas Jefferson, 24
    Parisian, 33
    slaves, 186
    social hierarchy, 48–49
coffee and coffeehouses, 2, 51–52, 186, 197
Colbert, Burwell, 140–41, 151
colonial cooking, 3–4, 157
Combeaux, 36, 37, 70, 202
de Conde, Prince, 110–11, 174
de Condorcet, Marquis, 21–22, 134, 163
Continental Congress, 25, 26, 171–72, 201
convents, 39–40, 60, 105, 121, 163
cookbooks, 64
    by men, 14–15, 61, 67
    by women, 3, 7, 112, 165–66, 191
Coolidge, Ellen Randolph, 140
cork and corkscrews, 89, 137, 174
corn, 5–6
correspondence (Thomas Jefferson)
    Abigail Adams, 42
    John Banister, 78

Mr Bellini, 53
Paul Bentalou, 45
Elizabeth Hemings, 37
Martha Jefferson (daughter), 12
Marquis de Lafayette, 82–83
Nicholas Lewis, 41
James Madison, 29, 130, 133, 141
James Monroe, 20–21, 78
Edward Rutledge, 95
William Short, 1, 78, 91–92
South Carolina Society for Promoting
    Agriculture, 97
Horatio Spafford, 120–21
Madame de Tesse, 88–89
Elizabeth House Trist, 128–29
George Washington, 148
Cosway, Maria, 114–15, 138, 163
Côte Rôtie, 89
crop failures, 72–73

Declaration of Independence, 25, 26, 161–62,
    171, 172, 201
dinner parties, 28
    Jefferson's in America, 146–47, 154–55,
        160
    Jefferson's in Paris, 113–18, 132–33, 134–
        36
    serving methods, 136, 150–51

emancipation, 35, 46, 151–53, 162, 203
Eppes family, 19, 99–102, 105, 162
Estates-General, 109–10, 123–25

figs, 11, 181
fish and shellfish, 4–5, 156. See also menus
florists, 74
food introductions, 3, 5–6, 185–90
food preparation, 75, 189–90
food shortages, 66, 135–36
Fossett family, 151, 155–56, 159, 186
France
    African population, 46
    colonies, 43–44, 71
    cuisine, 3, 6–7, 12–16, 61–63, 164–65
    drinking habits, 52–53
    government, 109–10, 123–25
    language, 19–20, 37–38, 40, 107–8
    provinces, 81
    roads, 79
    slavery laws, 43–46, 105–6
    social hierarchy, 48–49, 108–9

working poor, 82–83
    See also American Revolution; French
        Revolution; Paris
Franklin, Benjamin, 18, 25–31, 52, 55, 74
free blacks, 46
French fries, 116, 118
French Revolution, 122–33
    Jefferson on, 128–29, 131, 132, 145
    mobs and riots, 22, 51, 126–28, 130–32
    Reign of Terror, 51, 57
    roots of, 109–10
    sale of vineyards, 85
    victims of, 163
fried chicken, 189
frontier farms, 9
fruit
    African, 185–86
    figs, 11, 181
    orchards, 11–12

gardens
    Hôtel de Langeac, 41
    market, 59–60
    pleasure, 52
    slave-grown, 186
    Voltaire, 67
    See also Monticello
grain, 60–61, 72, 185–86. See also rice
grapes See wine
gumbo, 188

Hamilton, Alexander, 143–49, 203
Hannibal, 94–95
Harrison, William Henry, 165
Hemings, Elizabeth (Betty), 33–34, 37, 140,
    200, 201
Hemings, James
    apprenticeship, 35–37, 76, 110–13, 158,
        202
    Baltimore, 154, 158–59
    chef, 113–16, 149–54, 158–59, 204
    emancipation, 46, 151–53, 203
    familial connections, 33–34, 200
    French slave laws, 43–47
    language skills, 37–38, 121–22
    Monticello, 149–54, 158, 204
    New York City, 142–43
    Paris, 2, 20, 43–47, 58, 110–16
    Philadelphia, 152, 154, 203
    suicide, 164
Hemings, Martin, 151

Index

Hemings, Peter, 150–51, 186, 203
Hemings, Sarah (Sally), 102–8, 162, 202, 203
Henry, Patrick, 7, 157
The Hermitage, 90
Hern, David and Isabel, 102
holidays, 7–8, 13–14, 108, 186
hospitals, 126
Hôtel de Langeac, 41–42, 46, 86, 113–18
Hôtel d' Orléans, 22–24, 38
Hughes, Wormley, 180

illness and disease, 30, 54, 69, 72, 100, 106–7, 133–34
inoculation, 106–7
Invalides, 54, 127, 132
Italy, 93–96, 171, 202

Jay, John, 1, 120
Jefferson, Isaac, 103–4, 150
Jefferson, Lucy Elizabeth, 18–19, 99–101, 202
Jefferson, Martha (daughter), 201
    Atlantic crossings, 17, 19
    education, 10, 18, 38, 39–40
    in France, 19–20, 21, 24, 105, 202
    marriage, 162
    at Monticello, 139–41, 150, 203
    religious conversion, 119–21
Jefferson, Martha (wife), 10, 18, 34, 75, 170, 202
Jefferson, Mary, 202
    as adult, 162
    education, 10, 121
    with Eppes family, 18–19
    in France, 99–106
    return to Monticello, 203
Jefferson, Patsy See Jefferson, Martha (daughter)
Jefferson, Polly See Jefferson, Mary
Jefferson, Thomas
    accidents, 78
    account book, 19
    and Adams family, 32–33, 103, 154
    Atlantic crossings, 17, 19, 137–38
    and Benjamin Franklin, 30–31
    diet and food preferences, 2–3, 177–78, 181–83
    early life, 200
    education, 25, 171, 174, 200
    experiments, 11–12, 178–79
    in France, 19–21
    French Revolution, 128–29

French society, 42–43
    government service, 1–2, 12–13, 18, 52, 141–49, 202–4
    and Alexander Hamilton, 144–49
    inheritance, 34–35
    language skills, 17–18, 37–38
    Paris, 21–25, 32–33, 54–55, 57–58
    Paris home, 41–42, 46, 86, 113–18
    post-presidency, 161–65
    President, 57, 90, 154, 155–57, 204
    return to Monticello, 136–38, 140
    reunion with Polly, 99–105
    servants, 38, 42, 47–48, 77, 94, 104–5
    wine and wine tour, 77–98, 169–76, 202, 203
    writings, 86–87, 201, 202. see also Declaration of Independence
    See also correspondence (Thomas Jefferson); Monticello; slaves and slavery; specific Jefferson family members
Jenner, Edward, 107
Julien, Honoré, 155, 164, 188

kitchens
    American vs. French, 74–75
    colonial America, 74–75, 112–13
    French, 110–12
    Monticello, 150
kitchen utensils and equipment, 15, 112–13, 117, 137, 152, 174, 203

de Lafayette, Marquis
    American Revolution, 43, 54
    French Revolution, 132–33
    and Jefferson, 39, 56, 100, 135–36, 203
de La Rochefoucauld, Duke, 135, 163
de Launay, Bernard-René, 125–28
Lavoisier, Antoine, 21–22, 163
lawyers, 25
Lee, Arthur, 29, 31
Lee, Henry, 144
Lemaire, Étienne, 155–57, 164, 182–83, 188
lettuce, 182–83
Lewis and Clark Expedition, 11–12, 179, 181, 204
libraries, 131, 161, 204
Library of Congress, 116, 161, 191, 204
linens, 9
livestock, 11
Louisiana Territory, 11–12, 181, 204
Louis XIV

and French cuisine, 13–15
French Revolution, 122–25, 128, 135–36
Place Louis XIV, 51
support of American Revolution, 21, 29
See also Versailles
Louis XV, 14, 59, 62, 63–65
Louis XVI, 66, 73

macaroni and cheese, 116, 155, 196
Madeira, 170, 171–72, 200
Madison, Dolley, 140
Madison, James
and Alexander Hamilton, 146–47
and Thomas Jefferson, 29, 129, 130, 133,
140–41
and Henry Lee, 144
President, 161
Marin, François, 14–15, 61–62
Marseille, 92–93
Mazzei, Philip, 170–71, 174
McMahon, Bernard, 181–82
menus
Monticello, 150
plantation fare, 2–3, 7–9, 41
restaurant, 71–72
restorative, 68–69
royal, 13–15, 65, 66
See also dinner parties
Meursault, 85–86
Middle Ages, 21, 50, 55, 88, 108
monasteries, 60, 84–85, 92
Monticello
building of, 174, 201
cemetery, 101
gardens, 10–12, 178–84, 204
record books, 2, 184, 186, 187
return to, 136–39
sale of, 162
vineyard, 11, 12, 174–75
Morris, Gouverneur, 134–35

Nemeitz, Joachim, 69
New York City, 142–43
Nice, 94
Nîmes, 88

olives, olive oil, and olive trees, 97, 170–71,
183
orange trees, 32, 60, 94
orchards, 11–12, 178
d'Orléans, Duke, 71

palaces, 51. *See also* Versailles
Parent, Étienne, 42, 85
Paris
African population, 46
architecture, 21, 22, 50–51, 55
beggars, 20
feeding population, 59–61
food shops, 70
Middle Ages, 21, 50, 55, 108
squares, streets, and districts, 49–51
urban planning, 50–51
wall, 21–23, 123
working-class, 52–54
Parmentier, Antoine-Augustin, 73–74
pasta, 64, 113, 117, 174. *See also* macaroni and
cheese
pea, English, 181–82
Petit, Adrien, 42, 77, 94, 104–5
Philadelphia, 18, 143, 148, 152, 154
Pilgrims, 4–5
Place Louis XV, 51, 131
plantation fare, 2–3, 7–9, 41
plantations, 10, 33, 169–70, 200, 201. *See also*
Monticello
plant introductions, 11–12, 137, 170–71, 181,
183
de Pompadour, Madame, 63–64
Pontaille and Roze, 68–69
potato, 72–74, 116, 118
Potomac River, 143, 156
Protestants, 119–20
Provence, 81, 91–92
Puritans, 5, 25

Ramsey, Andrew, 103, 104, 105
Randolph family, 140, 162, 181–83, 188, 191
recipes
French, 115–18
James Hemings's, 158–59, 182–83, 198–99
Jefferson's, 2–3, 192–97
Monticello, 188–89
restaurants, 67–72
restoratives, 68–69, 91
Rhône River, 87–88
rice, 69, 93–95, 97–98, 202
riots, 22, 107, 126–28, 130–32
Roman architecture, 87–89, 91
Rousseau, Jean-Jacques, 15, 62–63
Roze and Pontaille, 68–69

INDEX

de Sade, Marquis, 125
salons, 28, 66, 109
sauces, 61–62
Sauternes, 42, 65
schools and colleges
American, 25, 161, 200, 204
English, 120
French, 39–40, 105, 121
science and scientists, 18, 21, 26, 107, 178–79
seasonings, 4, 7, 11
sesame, 183, 189
Short, William, 1, 78, 91–92
silk and silkworms, 33, 170–71
slaves and slavery
chefs/cooks, 3, 186
Burwell Colbert, 140–41, 151
diet, 5–6, 185–86
emancipation, 35, 46, 151–53, 162, 203
Edith and Peter Fossett, 151, 155–56, 159, 186
in France, 43–46, 105–6
David and Isabel Hern, 102
Wormley Hughes, 180
Isaac Jefferson, 103–4, 150, 179
slave owners, 6, 45. *See also* Jefferson, Thomas
See also specific Hemings family members
slums, 54, 109
smallpox, 106–7
Smollett, Tobias, 91
soil, 80, 83–84, 182
de Soubise, Prince, 61–62, 63
spas, 78, 91
stagecoaches, 79–80
strikes, 130–31

de Talleyrand, Charles, 135
taverns, 51–52, 69
taxation, 21–22, 122–23, 144
tobacco, 5–6, 184
tollhouses, 21, 22
tomato, 183
turkey, 6

U.S. Constitution, 120, 143
utensils, 9, 64, 203. *See also* kitchen utensils and equipment

Vacossin, Jean-François, 71–72
Van Buren, Martin, 165
vegetables

African, 185–86
Jefferson's favorites, 181–83
See also gardens
vegetarians, 15–16, 90
Versailles
meals at, 13–14
seat of government, 55–56
theater, 130
vineyards
French, 80–87, 89–90, 169
grand cru, 172
Hôtel de Langeac, 41
Monticello, 11, 12, 174–75
Voltaire, 52, 59, 64, 66–67

Washington (city), 148
Washington, George, 6, 25, 35, 141–42, 155, 203
Wayles, John, 33–34, 200, 201
wheat, 6, 73
The White House, 90, 116, 163, 164
wild game and game birds 5, 65–67, 90, 156
wine, 52–53, 68, 80, 89, 172
wine cellars, 82, 169–70
Wythe, George, 169, 171, 200

HUNGRY
FOR MORE?

VISIT
quirkbooks.com/foundingfoodie to:

* * *

View and download more recipes from
Thomas Jefferson and James Hemings

* * *

Discover contemporary
adaptations of these recipes

* * *

Read an interview with
author Thomas J. Craughwell

AND MUCH MORE!